Devastating

KU-736-704

The Neo-Conservative Assault on Democracy and Justice

Edited by Bernd Hamm

Pluto Press

LONDON • ANN ARBOR, MI

First published 2005 by Pluto Press
345 Archway Road, London N6 5AA
and 839 Greene Street, Ann Arbor, MI 48106

www.plutobooks.com

A slightly amended version of Chapter 4 was first published in Human Rights Watch's
2004 Report, and is reproduced with permission.
Chapter 6 was first published as chapters "The Revolt of the Bosses," and "Crime
Wave," in Ted Nace, *Gangs of America: The Rise of Corporate Power and the Disabling
of Democracy* (San Francisco Berrett-Koehler, 2003). Reprinted by permission of
Berrett-Koehler Publishing Company.
Chapter 9 © 2003 by Noam Chomsky; originally published in *New Political Science*,
Vol. 25, No. 1, 2003.
Chapter 10 first published as chapter 17 of William Blum, *Rogue State* (Monroe,
Maine: Common Courage Press, 2000), updated by and reprinted with permission of
the author.
Chapter 11 was first published in *Journal of International Affairs* (Columbia
University), vol. 52, no. 1 (Fall 1998); Center for Research on Globalization (CRG),
www.globalresearch.ca, 26 January 2002, and is reproduced with permission.

British Library Cataloguing in Publication Data
A catalogue record for this book is available from the British Library

ISBN   0 7453 2362 6 hardback
ISBN   0 7453 2361 8 paperback

Library of Congress Cataloging in Publication Data applied for

10   9   8   7   6   5   4   3   2   1

Designed and produced for Pluto Press by
Chase Publishing Services, Fortescue, Sidmouth, EX10 9QG, England
Typeset from disk by Stanford DTP Services, Northampton, England
Printed and bound in Canada by Transcontinental Printing

Contents

Abbreviations and Acronyms

9/11	September 11, 2001 attacks
ABC	American Broadcasting Corporation
ACLU	American Civil Liberties Union
ACSH	American Council on Science and Health
ACT	America Coming Together
AEI	American Enterprise Institute
AFL	American Federation of Labor
AFL-CIO	American Federation of Labor—Congress of Industrial Organizations
AI	Amnesty International
AIEDEP	African Institute for Economic Development and Planning
AIF	Animal Industry Foundation
AIPAC	American—Israel Public Affairs Committee
ALEC	American Legislative Exchange Council
ANC	African National Congress
ANWR	Arctic National Wildlife Reserve
AP	Associated Press
API	American Petroleum Institute
ASSC	Advancement of Sound Science Coalition
ATM	automatic teller machine
AU	Americans United for Separation of Church and State
BCCI	Bank of Credit and Commerce International
BCIS	Bureau of Citizenship and Immigration Services
BICE	Bureau of Immigration and Customs Enforcement
BIPAC	Business—Industry Political Action Committee
BNL	Banco Nazionale Del Lavoro
BOP	Bureau of Prisons
BSP	Bulgarian Socialist Party
CAREC	Clean Air Responsibility Enterprise Committee
CBS	Columbia Broadcasting System
CCSP	Climate Change Science Program
CD	Christian Democratic Party
CEO	Chief Executive Officer
CEQ	Council on Environmental Quality

CFACT	Committee for a Constructive Tomorrow
CFR	Council on Foreign Relations
CIA	Central Intelligence Agency
CLG	Citizens for Legitimate Government
CMA	Chemical Manufacturers Association
CNN	Cable News Network
CO_2	carbon dioxide
COINTELPRO	FBI's Counterintelligence Program
COW	Coalition of the Willing
CP	Communist Party
CREA	Council of Republicans for Environmental Advocacy
CRG	Center for Research on Globalization
DCI	Director of Central Intelligence
DEA	Drug Enforcement Administration
DHS	Department of Homeland Security
DNA	deoxyribonucleic acid
DPB	Defense Policy Board
DPG	Defense Planning Guidance
DRNK	Democratic Republic of North Korea
ECLAC	UN Economic Commission for Latin America and the Caribbean
ECO	Environmental Conservation Organization
ELN	National Liberation Army (Colombia)
ENN	Environmental News Network
EPA	Environmental Protection Agency
EPICA	Ecumenical Program in Central America and the Caribbean
EU	European Union
FAA	Federal Aviation Administration
FAIR	Fairness and Accuracy in Reporting
FARC	Revolutionary Armed Forces of Colombia
FASB	Financial Accounting Standards Board
FBI	Federal Bureau of Investigation
FCC	Federal Communications Commission
FEMA	Federal Emergency Management Agency
FISA	Foreign Intelligence Surveillance Act
FOE	Friends of the Earth
FOIA	Freedom of Information Act
FREE	Foundation for Research on Economics and the Environment
FWS	Fish and Wildlife Service

G7	Group of Seven (USA, Canada, Japan, UK, France, Germany, Italy)
G8	G7 plus Russia
GAO	General Accounting Office
GCC	Global Climate Coalition
GDP	Gross Domestic Product
GNP	Gross National Product
Group of 77	Developing countries in the UN
HCC	HCC Insurance Holdings Company
HHS	Health and Human Services
HMO	Health Maintenance Organization
HPI	Human Poverty Index
HRW	Human Rights Watch
HUD	US Department of Housing and Urban Development
IASPS	Institute for Advanced Strategic and Political Studies
ICBM	Intercontinental Ballistic Missile
ICCPR	International Covenant on Civil and Political Rights
ICRC	International Committee of the Red Cross
IFI	International Financial Institution
IMC	Independent Media Center
IMF	International Monetary Fund
INC	Iraqi National Congress
INS	Immigration and Naturalization Service
IPCC	Intergovernmental Panel on Climate Change
IRA	Irish Republican Army
ISI	Inter Services Intelligence
ITT	International Telephone and Telegraph
JINSA	Jewish Institute for National Security Affairs
LCV	League of Conservation Voters
LEC	Law and Economics Center
MAI	Multilateral Agreement on Investment
MPLA	Mozambique People's Liberation Army
MRI	magnetic resonance imaging
NAFTA	North American Free Trade Area
NAS	National Academy of Sciences
NATO	North Atlantic Treaty Organization
NBC	National Broadcasting Corporation
NCC	National Coal Council

NCTA	National Commission on Terrorist Attacks upon the United States
NED	National Endowment for Democracy
NEPDG	National Energy Policy Development Group
NGO	non-governmental organization
NIC	Newly Industrialized Country
NIMBY	not-in-my-back-yard
NMA	National Mining Association
NMCC	National Military Command Center
NORAD	North American Aerospace Defense Command
NRDC	Natural Resources Defense Council
NSA	National Security Advisor
NSC	National Security Council
NWF	National Wildlife Federation
NY	New York
OAU	Organization of African Unity
OECD	Organization for European Cooperation and Development
OFF	Oil for Food
OMB	Office of Management and Budget
OPEC	Organization of Petroleum Exporting Countries
OSHA	Occupational Safety and Health Administration
OSP	Office of Special Plans
PAC	Political Action Committee
PBS	Public Broadcasting Service
PEER	Public Employees for Environmental Responsibility
PLO	Palestine Liberation Organization
PNAC	Project for a New American Century
POGO	Project on Government Oversight
PSR	Physicians for Social Responsibility
S&B	Skull and Bones alumni
S&L	Savings and Loan
SAP	Structural Adjustment Program
SEC	Securities and Exchange Commission
SEPP	Science and Environmental Policy Project
SII	Sovereignty International Inc.
SLAPP	Strategic Lawsuit Against Public Participation
SOP	standard operational practice
SSA	Social Security Administration
SWAPO	South-West African People's Organization
TIA	Total Information Awareness
TNRCC	Texas Natural Resources Conservation Commission

UAE	United Arab Emirates
UBC	Union Banking Company
UDT	Timorese Democratic Union
UK	United Kingdom
UN	United Nations
UNDP	United Nations Development Program
UNESCO	United Nations Educational, Scientific and Cultural Organization
UNFPA	United Nations Population Fund
UNICEF	United Nations Children's Fund
UNITA	National Union for the Total Independence of Angola
UNRISD	United Nations Institute for Social Research and Development
UNSC	United Nations Security Council
US	United States
USAID	US Agency for International Development
USDA	United States Department of Agriculture
USGS	United States Geological Survey
USPIRG	US Public Interest Research Group
USSR	Union of Soviet Socialist Republics
USW	United Steel Works
VA	Veterans Affairs
WMDs	Weapons of Mass Destruction
WTC	World Trade Center
WTO	World Trade Organization
WWII	World War II

Preface

A large majority of all Europeans consider the United States government to be one of the most dangerous elements in global politics, according to a recent European opinion poll. So, it might not be too surprising that a European would want to initiate and edit a book which attempts to substantiate this negative perception of the only remaining superpower. Ever since World War II, the US has served as a role model for many in Europe, which had considerable impact on our societies. The aggressive, imperialistic side of US politics was usually ignored, and an alleged "community of values" postulated instead. The unilateral doctrine of the Bush administration broke this implicit consensus. Doubts about its legitimacy emerged after Greg Palast disclosed the presidential election fraud of 2000. There were reports of manipulated voting machines. At the time of writing it is difficult to know for certain if this will overshadow the election of 2004. The endless litany of the "world's oldest democracy" to which we owe solidarity and obedience has lost its persuasiveness.

For decades it had been relatively easy to foresee the future path of development—the closer European societies were allied to the US, the more would they follow the US pattern, and the correlation seemed to be tight. To understand where my own (German) society was heading, first of all I had to observe carefully the respective trends in the US. This is exactly what the book seeks to do. The result is frightening. Our political and economic leaders as well as the mainstream media must know that American society is deliberately and systematically devastated by the neo-conservative camarilla. Still, they tend to subserviently follow the dictates of the US government and the international financial and trade institutions it commands. Resistance is needed. We the people must make our governments understand that we don't want them to follow the US path. We should not give up basic moral standards. The International Court of Justice was set up after 1945 with the purpose of stopping major powers invading other people's countries and killing large numbers of their citizens. It is significant that the US government wishes today to ignore the International Court and not to be bound by its jurisdiction. There are now many people in the world who see that it is the US government who arbitrarily waged war on Iraq, lied to its own citizens and killed at least one hundred thousand Iraqi people. It seems that the age of mass murder has returned and this time it is the US and its allies who are responsible.

At the moment of writing, the US is governed by a group of right-wing war hawks with George W. Bush as their frontman; therefore I call this group the Bush Gang. To be very explicit: I have no commonality of values with the Bush Gang, but I do have common values with the authors of this book. This is not a normal, democratically legitimized government, and it should not be treated as if it were. The usual way university professors articulate their views is through writing or, in this case, editing books—while others organize protest rallies, engage with NGOs, boycott US products, or give back their Amexco credit cards, and some do all of these and more.

At first the book was envisaged for a non-American educated public to which it should provide a broad overview of the United States', and specifically the Bush Gang's, impact on the world, the Bush Gang's grab of power, and the effect this has on US society, and if copied, on others. In the ten months of discussions and writing, many of the authors found that although there is no lack of literature critical of the Bush Gang in the US, a book of this nature and comprehensiveness does not exist. Therefore it is also aimed at a US readership to which we apologize for a number of things all too familiar to them.

An outline was drafted of what such a book ideally would contain. Of course, this would have resulted in much too long a book. It was clear from the outset that I would not write this book myself—it would not only have gone beyond any competence of mine but also be immediately dismissed as being part of anti-Americanism. Its authors, therefore, should be mostly American. I contacted friends, posted the idea on mailing lists, and went to search the internet. In some cases articles could be found which were close to perfect to be included; here I asked for the permission to reproduce the chapter, in a few cases updated. Potential authors were solicited to contribute other chapters. The book is, on the one hand, critical of the power cadres in the US and the circles supporting them and, on the other hand, a sign of solidarity with the Other America.

Inevitably, of course, by this way of emergence the book carries also the perceptions and limitations of its editor for which the authors cannot be held responsible.

The first idea to initiate such a book evolved on a wonderful summer evening in the friendly company of German sociologist Fritz Vilmar— he is the first to thank. Fritz, and my wife Sabine and my friend and colleague Lydia Krüger, discussed several versions of the concept with me. I got helpful advice from, among others, Wendell Bell, Chip Berlet,

Herbert Gans, Ali Kazancigil, Ismail Lagardien, Michael Pugliese, Arno Tausch and Charles Tilly. Many encouraged the project without being able to cooperate, among them Wendell Bell, Luciana Bohne, Heather Boushey, William Hartung, Richard K. Moore, Greg Palast, Danny Schechter. Some, to whom I apologize, fell victim to the final cuts to allow the book to be published at a reasonable price. The email discussions with authors from abstracts via draft papers to final chapters was a rewarding experience and a real pleasure, a process of cooperation among people most of whom have never met face-to-face. I am grateful to all of them.

Bernd Hamm
Trier, Germany,
November 2004

Introduction

Bernd Hamm

Never since World War II have ordinary people found themselves so pitilessly pressed into job and income insecurity, never so unashamedly exploited by a small clique of shareholders and political and economic cadres (I deliberately eschew the term élite because it connotates the idea of moral superiority, which would definitely be misleading). Never have we been so openly deceived and dragged into wars in which thousands are slaughtered or crippled on the orders of someone who claims to be a Christian. Never was international law—the outstanding achievement of civilization—bypassed so self-righteously and cynically. Never has the common good, the basis of any democratic community, so hypocritically been attacked. Never has the Fourth Estate, the media, so utterly failed to fulfill their task of critically observing and reining in those in power. Never have fundamental civil rights been so restricted, and surveillance and repression become so all-encompassing. Never has public opinion been so perfectly manipulated. What sort of world is it where one family, allegedly the richest there is, has more assets than necessary to provide safe drinking water for every person in the world but does not care? The US Congress has approved a further $87.5 billion to continue the war against the people of Iraq. With this money, basic education for every child on earth could have been provided. It's a perverse world where the basic principles of social justice, democracy, and trust are lampooned.

It's globalization, stupid—or so they say. Some of the more enlightened would emphasize the role of global power structure, international financial speculation or neo-conservative ideology, while some of the less enlightened (including, alarmingly, many in so-called economic theory) refer to the alleged genetically determined greed of human nature. None of these theories, however, acts; only human beings do. It is not globalization that subjects drinking water or the energy supply to the demands of profit-making; nor does human nature privatize jails. This is why we focus on the top of today's global power hierarchy, that small group of people who wage war on others at will, who disdain the law if it is not to their benefit, who buy or depose other countries' governments, who create conditions in which their supporters amass immense fortunes while the majority of people live in poverty. The most visible element of this group sits in the US government and administration and because the frontman is the current president, George W. Bush, I call this group the Bush Gang. The Bush Gang extends far beyond the US. G8 (the eight most powerful industrial nations: the US, Canada, Japan, Germany, France, UK, Italy and Russia), the International Monetary Fund (IMF), the World Bank, the World Trade Organization (WTO), and military alliances such as NATO are the major instruments used to demand loyalty worldwide.

Long before the Bush Gang, successive US governments rarely hesitated to enforce their claim to power by means of overt or covert action, but none has been as ruthless as the Bush Gang. It was only recently that some of the traditional vassals showed tentative signs of opposition: Canada, Germany, France, and Belgium did not answer the Bush Gang's call to war against Iraq, but many did (COW, the 'coalition of the willing'), mostly against the wishes of the overwhelming majority of their populations. Six million people around the world rallied in protest against the war on February 15, 2003. I admit that for a brief moment I dreamed we would succeed. We did not. Iraq was bombed to rubble, its infrastructure destroyed, its people left without water, electricity, and petrol. Meanwhile, the Bush Gang is selling Iraqi oil to its friends—oil desperately needed to fuel Iraqi power plants and water works. While 60 per cent of Iraqis are unemployed, US-based corporations awarded billion-dollar contracts for reconstruction hire cheap immigrant workers. This is how hatred is generated.

The tentacles of the Bush Gang touch on many aspects of daily life, not only in the US, but also abroad. Political and economic advisors can be found not only in the transition countries of Eastern Europe, via the IMF and its structural adjustment dictates they are in direct control of the economic policy of the majority of the world's countries. The OECD and IMF regularly give advice on how the economic policy of allied countries should be drafted. With the help of the WTO, neoliberal principles, deregulation, and privatization are pushed through. Often, their influence is indirect and difficult to detect. Public opinion manipulation, i.e. propaganda industries, booms. The media, which excel at advertising, circulation, and market shares, and are increasingly dedicated to infotainment, are not helpful in providing orientation for ordinary people. Better and more reliable information is restricted to those who have the time, knowledge, and motivation to spend hours on daily information gathering.

One of the most telling examples can be seen in the "compelling evidence" provided by US Secretary of State Colin Powell to the UN Security Council on February 5, 2003 on Iraq's weapons of mass destruction. Even as it was being presented, interested internet users around the world knew that the document tabled was a fake, copied from a student's paper twelve years out of date without even correcting for typing errors. The German foreign minister, Joschka Fischer, once a political activist and Vietnam war protestor, had the gall to call this so-called evidence convincing. There have been few events as unashamed as that.

In fact, the Bush Gang is an epiphenomenon we are observing and, in part, analysing. The underlying cause is a *system* which allowed the Bush Gang to seize power, throttle US society, and wage war on other countries. What is this system? And how does it work?

From the Great Depression up to the mid-1970s there was a broad consensus in all Western societies and across almost the entire political spectrum that economic growth was the primary goal and that the surplus gained by growth should (a) be distributed among the working population in the form of wage increases and social security, and the owners, (b) used to repair ecological damage brought about by growth, and (c) given to developing countries. The underlying conviction was that we can thrive only if all thrive. This was the social democratic, or Keynesian, consensus, and could be achieved only if two prerequisites were in place: a booming economy, and a relatively balanced power structure.

In the mid-1970s a sudden and unforeseen alignment of events shattered this consensus. It included the end of the Vietnam war; the first oil price shock and energy crisis; rising energy prices and interest rates, leading to the beginning of the international debts crisis; the onset of unemployment in the OECD countries; the abandonment by the US government of the Bretton Woods currency system and the transition to floating exchange rates; the end of the decolonization process and with it the new weight of the Group of 77 in the UN General Assembly; the stillborn New World Economic Order in the United Nations; the withdrawal of the US from the International Labour Organization (ILO) (and later from UNESCO); the beginning of the G7; the end of the US paying its UN dues; the Stockholm World Conference on the Environment; the Club of Rome report, *The Limits to Growth*; major technological innovations like glass fiber, the microchip, and the spread of personal computers; the internet; the isolation of DNA sections and the beginning of genetic manipulation; and the CIA-instigated *coup d'état* in Chile and assassination of its president, Salvador Allende. With the changing majority in the UN General Assembly as a consequence of decolonization, the US, together with its Western allies, began systematically to dismantle the UN (witness the use of the veto in the Security Council, or the refusal to accept the International Court of Justice's rulings, e.g. on the mining of the Nicaraguan ports, and the political blackmailing of the UN against the payment of only a part of regular dues) and the construction of a parallel, informal, undemocratic global power structure—the G7. It was also the beginning of the end of the socialist regimes, largely brought about by foreign debt.

Today's G8, dominated and led by the US, controls the Security Council (except China), the IMF, the World Bank, the WTO, and NATO (with its new mandate based on common interests instead of common territory), which together will be referred to as the G8 institutions. Even if they are led by the US government, the other seven are responsible fellow travelers. The logic behind all of this is the will to secure access to natural resources for the benefit of the West at the cost of accelerating deprivation, especially of the developing countries. The Western coalition was indifferent because all cadres were well aware that their political support at home relies on the assurance of ever-continuing growth. Real exponential growth in the wealthy countries, however, can only be achieved at the expense of the developing countries, further depriving the working class, and continuing deterioration of the global life support system. This is a fact beyond statistical sleights of hand such as the hedonic pricing in US GNP accounting, and despite decades-old criticism of growth as an index of welfare.

An interesting new element is that, for the very first time since WWII, the Afghanistan and Iraq wars have split the Western coalition. It would come as no surprise if dissent within the G8 institutions increased, as is already the case within NATO. It is an illusion to believe that NATO can be extended further eastwards and still be governed single-handedly.

The G8 institutions all work under strictly executive order—thereby excluding any legislative or judiciary control. At the same time there is economic concentration in a handful of huge conglomerates called transnational corporations. Together they rule out democratic decision-making and the idea of organizing society from the bottom up. Global cadres have taken over. An interesting, though little known, example is the Carlyle Group which brings together, among an interesting number of others, the Bush and bin Laden families, as well as the Russian oligarch Mikhail Chodorkovsky, who was detained in Siberia at the very moment he was intending to sell the majority of the Russian oil giant Yukos to Exxon Mobile. Some conspiracy theorists go as far as to assume that the energy crisis was planned at a meeting of the Bilderberg

Group in May 1973 on the Swedish island of Salstjöbaden.[1] Whatever the case, it is naive to assume that world political and economic leaders never meet to exchange and coordinate views in places like the Davos World Economic Forum, or privately, however and wherever they wish. They will certainly do everything in their power to protect themselves from the incalculable coincidence of democratic decision-making. Some dismiss this as a conspiracy theory. However, the facts supporting it are there for all to see. The only real conspiracy theory is the one maintaining against all the evidence that Osama bin Laden was behind the 9/11 attacks.

Since the mid-1970s, unemployment and rising welfare costs have burdened already indebted states. The beginning of the abandonment of the welfare state and Keynesian policies led, in the early 1980s, to neo-conservative governments in the UK, US, Germany and later other countries. The mid-1970s also witnessed a change in power relations. On a world scale, Western capitalist countries successfully defeated, and began to bring under their control, the developing countries. This *second colonization* was largely based on "structural adjustment" whereby other countries were subjugated, and according to neo-conservative ideology Keynesian redistribution was turned upside down within the rich countries. On a national scale, unemployment and political strategy helped to undermine the trade unions as the major plank of Keynesian politics. Public opinion was gradually turned away from social democratic models, which were accused of creating the crisis, and towards conservative "supply-side" and neo-conservative concepts. Capital markets were "liberalized." The coming to office of the neo-conservative governments in 1979/80 strengthened this process which had begun under social democratic rule.

The final neo-conservative takeover after 1990 was made possible by five interacting elements. *Neo-conservatism* was promoted by right-wing US think tanks; the so-called *Nobel Prize for Economics*; the *Washington Consensus*; the *collapse of the socialist regimes,* and the *dismantling of the trade unions* in the West worked together to produce a climate in which only market fundamentalism seemed to offer solutions to socio-economic problems. While we used to criticize the exclusively Marxist understanding of science in the socialist countries, we failed to notice the extent to which our own systems had been brainwashed and underwent an epistemological cleansing after 1989.

(1) Right-wing think tanks succeeded in framing public opinion along conservative lines. George Lakoff and his colleagues at Rockridge Institute[2] analysed the decades-long efforts of right-wing think tanks and foundations to form public opinion and push through the

neo-conservative agenda. Lakoff, like others before him, discerns two major worldviews.

The *conservative worldview* is basically authoritarian and, hierarchical. The state is like the traditional family: the president governs and has the right to expect discipline and obedience in the same way that a father rules his family and expects discipline and obedience from his children. Disobedience is met with physical punishment. The world is evil; father protects and needs the means to protect. He is the moral authority; whatever he does is right. Traditional power relations are a guide to morality: God above man, man above nature, adults above children, western culture above non-western culture, America above other nations. (There are also bigoted versions: straights above gays, Christians above non-Christians, men above women, whites above non-whites.) The US is seen as more moral than other nations and hence more deserving of power. It has the right to be hegemonic and must never yield its sovereignty or its overwhelming military and economic power. It is God's own country, populated by the chosen people, and, surrounded by potential misbelievers and enemies. Father/president/US must never yield their authority over others. Patriotism is exclusive; it means loyalty to one's own group and to government only if it belongs to one's own group. Thus, patriotism can go hand in glove with discrimination against minorities. Material success is a mark of superior morality. Lack of success indicates less moral strength and less discipline. Pursuit of self-interest is moral—if everybody pursues their own self-interest, then the interest of all will be maximized.

As a political doctrine, the conservative worldview translates into support for capital punishment, tough law-and-order measures, opposition to welfare spending, less taxation and economic regulation, puritanical and hypocritical attitudes towards sexuality, and finally, a strong national defense so that enemies can be punished appropriately.[3] Consider the Project for a New American Century (PNAC) for an exact translation of this view into a political program which became enacted as the National Security Strategy.[4]

This is what many non-Americans perceive as the pre-enlightenment, dark, retrograde, uncivilized, stuffy image of US society, the one of the National Rifle Association, the Bible Belt, the death penalty, anti-abortionism, racism and discrimination, paired with self-righteousness and paranoia. Historians will recall the Calvinist ethos which led to terror in sixteenth-century Geneva, and sociologists will think of Theodor Adorno's famous research on the authoritarian personality,[5] or of Johan Galtung's DMA syndrome: **D**ualist, the world is divided into US(A) and them; there are no neutrals; **M**anichean, our party is good, their party is evil; and Armageddon, there can be only one outcome, the final battle.[6]

In contrast, the *progressive/liberal worldview* sees the world as a nurturing place, which is to be protected. While the family is a place of intimacy and mutual care, the state is the place where different ideologies and interests meet to negotiate rational solutions to complex problems in the pursuance of the common good. Theoretically, the common good can be defined as the situation where nobody can exercise his or her liberty to the detriment of anyone else (another formulation of the "Pareto optimum" of economic theory). Human beings differ, though they are of equal right, and are all entitled to the pursuit of happiness and social participation. Empathy and responsibility are the core concepts, with many consequences: responsibility implies protection, competence, education, hard work, and social engagement. Empathy requires fairness and honesty, open, two-way communication, a happy, fulfilled life, and restitution rather than retribution to balance the moral books. The role of government is to care for and protect the population, especially those who are helpless and inarticulate, to guarantee democracy (the equal sharing of power), to promote well-being and ensure justice for all. The economy should be a means to these moral ends.[7] Patriotism here is inclusive and means loyalty to the founding constitutional principles. If the government violates these principles, it is not only one's right, but also one's duty to criticize, oppose and, if necessary, resist government.

This is the open, democratic, cultured, just US society so often praised and admired by non-Americans. Its foresight, fairness, and intellect have brought it to help found the United Nations and draw up the Charter of Human Rights. It is this US which maintains global solidarity and sustainable development. It is conscious of the fact that it has only one voice in the family of nations. When it leads, it does so with modesty, tolerance, rational argument, and sympathy for all.

The question, central to humankind, was which soul in the US body would prevail over the other. With the Bush Gang, the conservative fraction has taken over all four powers: the legislative, the executive, the judiciary and the media.

Starting in the 1960s and accelerating in the 1970s, conservative intellectuals worked to fashion a political ideology that would allow the different conservative groups to coalesce under a single umbrella. The stratagem that intellectuals used to reconcile the conflicting viewpoints of religious and economic conservatives was to treat "the market" as akin to a divine force that always calls for moral behavior. They sought to expunge the lessons of the Great Depression from collective memory.

Religious and economic conservatives together sold Americans the quack medicine of untrammeled free markets and the glorification of *greed is good*. Over the last 25 years, the consequence has been a collapse of business ethics: infectious greed has been institutionalized in corporate suites. Excessive salaries, the manipulation of balance sheets, and the avoidance of taxes are now all too familiar. At the same time, regulatory institutions are in a state of disarray because the free market mantra insists that regulation is illegitimate and unnecessary.[8] Today, the Bush Gang's war against Iraq has succeeded in pushing corporate scandals off the frontpage.

Conservative institutions like the Olin or Heritage Foundations and their think tanks have framed virtually every issue in their perspective. They have invested billions of dollars in changing ideas and language. They have set up professorships and institutes on and off campus where intellectuals write books from a conservative business perspective. Conservative foundations give large block grants year after year to these think tanks. They build infrastructure and TV studios, hire intellectuals, set aside money to buy large quantities of books to get them on the bestseller lists, hire research assistants for their intellectuals so they can perform well on TV, and hire agents to get them on TV. They produce manuals which, issue after issue, present what the logic of the position is from a conservative side, what the opponent's logic is, how to attack it, and what language to use. Along these lines, George W. Bush was framed and sold as a "compassionate conservative." Susan George[9] has provided data on how neo-conservative ideology was manufactured, and how it spread across the US and Europe: "The doctrines of the International Monetary Fund, the World Bank, and the World Trade Organization are indistinguishable from those of the neo-conservative credo." She concurs with Lakoff in her analysis that right-wingers, by funding institution-building, have become incredibly more successful than project-oriented progressives in shaping public opinion.[10]

In reality, however, the state was not dismantled but rather used by capital to reduce its tax burden while relying more and more on taxes squeezed from lower income groups, privatization of public assets, deregulating certain areas, e.g. energy, safeguarding offshore tax havens, and channelling more money than ever into the military-industrial complex, transferring the economic surpluses from labor to finance, and pressing other governments to finance the trade balance deficit. Whereas the markets for goods can become saturated, or fail to extract profit because of an absence of purchasing power, the military is insatiable as long as new technologies are being developed and implemented, and wars deliberately waged to destroy the "goods" delivered. The

French historian Emmanuel Todd explains why US governments have always attacked relatively small and helpless countries like Grenada, Nicaragua, Libya, Cuba, Afghanistan, and Iraq. By this demonstration of "strength," faith in the dollar as the world reserve currency could be maintained, an instrument of power which is endangered by the double deficit of the budget and the trade balance.[11]

In short, with immeasurably more money, better organization, more fervent comittment, and finally the *coup d'état* of the November 2000 presidential elections, the conservative worldview seized power and is now perfecting its control to an extent that makes some fear the emergence of a new fascism.

(2) The *Nobel Prize for Economics* can be seen as part of this venture. Very few people are aware that no such thing exists in reality. Rather, what has become known as the Nobel Prize for Economics is the "Prize of the Bank of Sweden for Economics in Memory of Alfred Nobel" and is neither funded from Nobel's fortune (but by the Bank of Sweden) nor awarded according to the same rules and procedures as the genuine Nobel prizes. This is important because of the prestige Nobel prizes command as the most authoritative recognition worldwide in their respective fields. Despite the thousands of university chairs in economics around the world, since the inauguration of the prize in 1969 40 out of 51 Laureates have been US citizens or work in the US, nine of them at the University of Chicago alone; ten prizes were awarded to economists in Western Europe, just one to a Third World economist, and none to the East—an outcome not very likely from simple statistical probability theory. The man most influential in selecting Economics Laureates has been the Swedish economist Assar Lindbeck. In 1994 he published a book entitled *Turning Sweden Around*, which called for drastic cutbacks in Sweden's welfare state.[12] As Lindbeck has turned neoliberal, so has the selection of prize winners:

> Between 1990 and 1995, the Nobel has gone to someone from the University of Chicago five out of six times. What is the relationship between Lindbeck and the University of Chicago? By all accounts, it is a cozy one. ... For example, Lindbeck joined Nobel laureates Milton Friedman, Gary Becker, and Douglas North in a long-running project to construct an "Economic Freedom Index." The purpose of this project was to rank developing nations by the level of government interference in their economies. It was funded by the Center for International Private Enterprise, a far-right think tank

designed to promote the international business interests of its affiliate, the U.S. Chamber of Commerce.[13]

(3) The *Washington Consensus*, and with it structural adjustment policy, began long before John Williamson published his "Ten Commandments" (1990) as the "lowest common denominator of policy advice being addressed by the Washington-based institutions to Latin American countries as of 1989."[14] In another article he admitted that while he invented the term "Washington Consensus," he did not invent its content but rather "*reported* accurately on opinions in the international financial institutions and the central economic agencies of the U.S. government" (emphasis added).[15] Williamson distanced himself on several occasions from treating the term as a synonym for neoliberalism, or market fundamentalism, to be imposed on developing countries. But he also left no doubt that he had never argued for "giving socialism another chance."[16] It never was what the name suggests: a consensus reached following negotiations between rich and poor countries to reduce poverty and the foreign debt burden. It was not even an explicit agreement among the rich country majority of the International Financial Institutions (IFIs), but rather tacitly supported. If one asked an informed member of one of its victim societies, it was bitterly criticized as the devilish medicine imposed on developing countries to deprive them of their natural resources, to prevent their development and self-determination, and keep them in poverty. Here is one of these voices:

> The "Consensus" was drawn up by a group of economists, officials of the U.S. Government, the World Bank and the International Monetary Fund. A very restricted consensus; it was never the subject of general debate and never submitted to a vote. It was not even formally ratified by the countries it was imposed on. It has been, and still is, an authoritarian exercise, greedy and unsupportive, whose champions try to justify it on the grounds of the supposedly unquestionable economic-scientific character of its guidelines. ... Latin America, the principal victim of the "Consensus," is a prime example for the disaster it has caused. In 1980 there were 120 million poor; in 1999 the number had increased to 220 million, 45 % of the population. ... After a decade of blindly devoted application of the Washington Consensus guidelines, Latin America stands at the edge of a precipice. Debt grew from U.S.$ 492,000 million in 1991 to U.S.$ 787,000 million in 2001. Railways, telecommunications, airlines, drinking water supplies and energy supplies were virtually

wound up and handed over to giant U.S. and European corporations. Public spending on education, health, housing and social benefits was reduced, price control was abolished, wages were frozen and millions of workers were dismissed by the new masters of the now-privatised public undertakings.[17]

He found it paradoxical that, "while the world's physicists call into question the immovable and unquestionable nature of certain principles of Science (with a capital) editors, defenders and executors of the ill named 'Washington Consensus' claim that this selfish, obscene and biased view of the economy is pure economic science, making compliance obligatory. The 'Consensus', however, used to predict that with its application economic growth would increase, poverty would diminish and employment would expand. Just the opposite. Moreover, intensive use of natural resources has caused damage, perhaps irreparable damage, to the environment."[18]

Former World Bank senior vice president and chief economist Joseph Stiglitz criticized the way in which a uniform neo-conservative version of the Washington Consensus was imposed on indebted countries. Stiglitz acknowledged that in most countries subjected to structural adjustment, and especially in the transition countries of Eastern Europe and the former Soviet Union, the more or less uniformly applied medicine did not reduce poverty and income/wealth polarization, nor did it reduce the debt burden or lead to economic or environmental stabilization.[19] Going one step further, Michel Chossudovsky[20] accused the IMF and WTO of being the cause of terrible poverty, exploitation, and war. "O'Neill's Treasury Department controls the most powerful institutions that enforce the rules of the Washington Consensus: the IMF and the World Bank. Our government also has the biggest voice in the WTO, whose rules are widely seen as stacked against developing countries."[21]

Summarizing, the expected consequences of the victory for "American values" at the WTO are: (1) a "new tool" for far-reaching US intervention into the internal affairs of others; (2) the takeover of a crucial sector of foreign economies by US-based corporations; (3) benefits for business sectors and the wealthy; (4) shifting of costs to the general population; (5) new and potentially powerful weapons against the threat of democracy.[22]

In blaming the US Treasury and the US-led IFIs, we should not forget, however, that the G8 countries *combined* hold the majority of votes, so they are complicit. As they are usually represented by their finance ministers and central bank presidents in the IFI executive bodies, we should not be surprised to find little understanding, interest, or empathy for the harm done to others.

(4) Fourth, the *collapse of the socialist regimes*. This is not the place to recapitulate how and under which internal and external circumstances this occurred. Nor can we discuss here how much average Americans knew of really existing socialism. However, it is evident that this event was followed, in all Western and Eastern European countries, by a process of *epistemological cleansing*. Socialist regimes, so the argument goes, failed because, among other reasons, they had been based on theoretical foundations which, by the time of the collapse, had become empirically untenable. Therefore, Marxist thinking had been proved false and had to be eradicated, and with it all leftist and dialectical approaches. Intellectually impoverished as the argument might be, it swept through the schools and universities and across the media, and served to extinguish or at least totally marginalize troublesome thinking. Thus, the epistemological spectrum in economics today is characterized by an overwhelming majority of neo-conservatives, plus some Keynesian economists which might go under the rubric of "repressive tolerance," to borrow an expression of Herbert Marcuse. In the perception of the political sphere and the media as well as of the public, economics became homogenized to serve the ideological interests of the rich and applaud the deprivation of the poor. Paradoxically enough, the victory of Western-style democracy and open competition of ideas and opinions over alleged streamlined socialist ideology has led to the silencing of most critical voices, and the streamlining of thought along crypto-capitalist lines. The intellectual brainwashing was most successful in the Eastern European transition countries. Although people there should be more informed and skeptical about the benefits of capitalism, their naïveté and innocent beliefs are surprising and easy to exploit.

(5) We should not forget, in addition, the *decline of the trade unions* a process that could be observed shortly after the conservatives came to power in the early 1980s. Ronald Reagan, after passing a number of anti-union Acts, used the military to break up the air traffic controllers' strike; Margaret Thatcher aggressively privatized the highly unionized public sector services. In Germany, the unions fouled themselves, beginning with scandalous corruption in union-owned cooperatives such as Neue Heimat and Coop. These incidents, together with rising unemployment, resulted in declining strike funds and massive losses

of union membership and, therefore, of bargaining power. So it was not difficult to push through the agenda of "supply-side economics" after blaming Labour/the Democrats/the Social Democrats for being responsible for the recession. Coordinated or not, the coincidence is eye-catching; the first soft version of neo-conservatism had arrived.

Once the redistribution pattern was reversed from top down and bottom up with the help of privatization, cutbacks in the social welfare system, and tax relief for the rich, the process of ideological brainwashing became self-reinforcing. The immense wealth accumulated in just a few hands was used for currency and stock speculation, for blackmailing national governments in order to gain further tax cuts and for the ideological tuning of the media, the political sphere, and public opinion. It went smoothly: opposition was close to non-existent or incorporated. It is true but relatively unimportant to the powerful cadres that domestic purchasing power falls; overproduction goes into exports and destroys employment in the importing countries—they make money out of money. It is much more important to gain control of the media and public opinion, and thus of the electorate. Silvio Berlusconi in Italy and Rupert Murdoch in Australia and the US have been most successful in demonstrating how this can be achieved. This should, however, not divert attention from the covert action of the propaganda machine. Ultimately, the state is transformed into an instrument serving the wishes of CEOs and shareholders. The degree to which US governments, and especially the Bush Gang, have rewarded their sponsors with influential positions and lucrative contracts is, in the eyes of most Europeans, deeply corrupt.[23] With decreasing real income and a heavy debt burden, the state dismantles itself and the social security system with it. Deregulation is not much more than a shift from distributionary towards repressive instruments, and privatization is the final desolate measure to plug holes in the budget while, at the same time, taking away even more regulatory power from democratically controlled institutions.

It is only in this frame of reference that the stolen presidential election of November 2000 and the power grab by the PNAC group can be explained. In this light, 9/11 was instrumental in creating fear among the general public, to increase consent for the president and the government and the repressive measures they enacted, and to deliver arguments for aggression against others. The blueprint, once again, came from a right-wing think tank, the Olin Foundation, with Samuel Huntington's article, and then his book on the *Clash of Civilizations*.[24] Everywhere in the capitalist world an unprecedented propaganda campaign was launched against Arabs and Muslims ("Islamophobia," a campaign very similar to anti-Semitism). It is amazing to observe how much attention the media pay to the arrest of alleged terrorists, and how little they take note later of their release due to lack of evidence. Democratic opposition was intimidated and silenced, and democratic standards of transparency and checks and balances displaced. Here the US is once again the trendsetter followed, though not with the same rigidity, by other governments. The consequences can easily be observed in growing income and wealth polarization, and increasing tension, violence, and repressive reaction in US society. The spill-over to other countries is difficult to ignore.

> Naturally the common people don't want war ... but after all, it is the leaders of the country who determine policy, and it is always a simple matter to drag the people along, whether it is a democracy, or a fascist dictatorship, or a parliament, or a communist dictatorship ... All you have to do is to tell them they are being attacked, and denounce the pacifists for lack of patriotism and exposing the country to danger. It works the same in any country—so said Herman Goering at the Nuremberg Trials.

The Bush Gang follows this prescription to the letter.

Most bewildering is the almost complete lack of public outcry against such policies. While the Bush Gang seems to be fully committed to serving the rich, and above all its sponsors, it is surprising to see that most of its supporters are those who stand to lose the most from virtually all their policies: blue-collar workers: 49 per cent of men and 38 per cent of women told a January 2003 Roper poll they would vote for Bush in 2004. Blue-collar workers represent 55 per cent of all voters, a fact that has not been lost on Republican strategists. The more precarious and difficult their job and income situation is, the more they seem to favor the conservative worldview and call for strong leadership. Republican rhetoric seems to appeal precisely to this group. Humiliation and fear can easily be transformed into anger if one manages to point a finger at the guilty: minorities, immigrants, women, terrorists. The Republicans are clearly doing all they can to direct that anger away from the beneficiaries of Bush's policies. "Paired with this is an aggressive right-wing attempt to mobilize blue-collar fear, resentment, and a sense of being lost—and attach it to the fear of American vulnerability, American loss. By doing so, Bush aims to win the blue-collar man's identification with big business, empire, and himself."[25]

Thus, the system which has brought the Bush Gang to power was systematically prepared a long time ago and bore fruit long before George W. Bush was selected for the White House by the Supreme Court on December 12, 2000. It is this system which we set on to analyse in this book.

Part I analyses the power cadres. William Bowles, in "Bush Family Saga," demonstrates to what extent the Bush family, criminal as it might appear to be, is no more than an epiphenomon of the US capitalist system, the unculture of robber barons. This view is extended in Andrew Austin's analysis of the "War Hawks." In the final chapter of Part I, Walter E. Davis summarizes the evidence on whether or not the power cadres might have been complicit in the 9/11 attacks.

Part II illustrates some of the aspects in which US society is affected. It starts with Alison Parker's and Jamie Fellner's analysis of the human rights situation after 9/11. Domestic economic problems and their ramifications are described by Trevor Evans. Ted Nace sets out to investigate criminal behavior within big US corporations. Jay Shaft gives an account of poverty and homelesness after the Bush Gang came to office. While Evans' assessment is very much based on official statistics, Shaft has invested a lot of effort to go beyond these. His chapter is also remarkable for its compassion for the victims of the Bush gang, which shines through the numbers he reports. Andrew Austin's and Laurel Phoenix's chapter on the "Rise of Anti-Environmentalism" demonstrates how the Bush Gang is damaging the common good of all Americans; furthermore, because the US is by far the greatest consumer of global natural resources, its neglect of environmental policy must be seen as yet another act of aggression against the rest of the world.

Part III brings together arguments describing the US as the world hegemon, how it works, and with what consequences. It is introduced by Noam Chomsky's broad account of US-led wars of terror. In his "Concise History of US Global Interventions," William Blum documents the overt and covert acts of aggression successive US governments have inflicted on other countries. For a full picture, interventions by means of diplomacy and, especially important, through the IMF and its debt management should be added. Michel Chossudovsky gives an account of world poverty and how it is related to US policies.

The final Part is an attempt to find, after the foregoing desolate analyses, a positive element of resistance: Laurel Phoenix provides an overview of the diverse scenario of dissenting groups and movements.

While this provides a broad view, there is a lot more ground which is impossible to cover in a single book. To mention only some of the issues which could have been included here:

- The real history of the United States, which was always based on aggression, intolerance, and the rule of a small clique who were successful in convincing people that this is democracy, while in fact ruthlesly following their own egoistic interest.
- The changing history of United States—UN relations, from the Anti-Hitler coalition to Richard Perle's "Thank God for the death of the UN."
- The intricate relations between the US Treasury, Wall Street, the IMF, World Bank, and WTO.
- The loss of institutional democratic opposition as analysed in Robert Kuttner's eye-opening article on America as a One-Party State.[26]
- The change in daily life since 9/11 in the experience of ordinary people; the fear created by repeatedly announcing terrorist threats; and the surveillance and intimidation of democratic expression.[27]
- The use made by the US government of propaganda, "public opinion management," "strategic communication," and the machinations of the propaganda industries.
- Homeland Security, Patriot Acts 1 and 2, Total Information Awareness, and other attempts to restrict civil liberties, including pressure on other countries to follow the US model.
- Government by presidential Executive Order, or governance without transparency.
- The role of religion in shaping government and public opinion, and how religion becomes distorted to serve the interestes of the power cadres.
- The deterioration of public infrastructure including social welfare, education,[28] and health services, as well as public transportation, water, and energy[29] supplies.
- The Pentagon and the military industrial complex having metamorphosed over time to create the most lethal killing institution the world has ever seen.
- The commercial worldview, carried to its extreme in the US, leaving only commercial or exchange value.
- Cultural and linguistic imperialism in its many facets, from advertising via popular music and fast food to fashion, sports and Hollywood movies.[30]

It is easy to see that there is enormous scope for many more urgently needed analyses on the way to a truly comprehensive picture. This book may encourage others to look beyond single, isolated issues and contribute to a more thorough understanding.

NOTES

1. F. W. Engdahl, *A Century of War: Anglo-American Oil Politics and the New World Order* (Wiesbaden: Boettiger, 1992), pp. 205–7.
2. See www.rockridgeinstitute.org; also Joan Roelofs, *Foundations and Public Policy – The Mask of Pluralism* (Albany, NY: SUNY, 2003); and Jerry M. Landay: "The Apparat," http://www.mediatransparency.org /stories/apparat.html.
3. G. Lakoff, *Moral Politics* (Chicago Ill.: University of Chicago Press, 1996); see also G. Lakoff, "Metaphor, Morality, and Politics, or, Why the Conservatives Have Left Liberals in the Dust," *Social Research*, vol. 62, no. 2 (Summer 1995).
4. "Project for a New American Century: Rebuilding America's Defense" www.newamericancentury.org/RebuildingAmericasDefense.pdf.
5. T. W. Adorno et al., *Studies in Prejudice* (New York: Harper & Brothers, 1950).
6. J. Galtung, "Exiting from the Terrorism–State Terrorism Vicious Cycle: Some Psychological Conditions," Acceptance Speech, Morton Deutsch Conflict Resolution Award, Chicago, August 25, 2002.
7. Lakoff, "Metaphor," p. 11.
8. B. A. Powell, "How Right-Wing Conservatives Have Hijacked U.S. Democracy," www.berkeley.edu/news/media/releases/2003/10/27_lakoff.shtml.
9. S. George, "How to Win the War of Ideas?" *Dissent*, vol. 44, (Summer 1997): pp. 47–53.
10. See also, in a broader perspective on foundations, J. Roelofs, *Foundations and Public Policy: The Mask of Pluralism* (Albany, NY: SUNY, 2003).
11. E. Todd, *Après l'empire. Essai sur la décomposition du système américain* (Paris: Gallimard, 2002).
12. A. Lindbeck et al., *Turning Sweden Around* (Camdridge Mass.: MIT Press, 1994).
13. D. Bashford, email, January 7, 2001, to the Ecological Economics list.
14. J. Williamson, "What Should the World Bank Think about the Washington Consensus?" *The World Bank Research Observer*, vol. 15, no. 2, (2000) pp. 251–64.
15. Ibid.
16. J. Williamson, "Did the Washington Consensus Fail?" Institute for International Economics (November 6, 2002).
17. C. X. Tamayo, "Burying the 'Washington Consensus'." Agencia de Informacion Solidaria, February 26, 2003 (translated by Prudence Dwyer), www.globalpolicy.org/socecon/bwi-wto/imf/2003/0226bury.html.
18. Ibid.
19. J. Stiglitz, *Globalization and its Discontents* (New York: Norton, 2002).
20. M. Chossudovsky, *The Globalization of Poverty* (Penang: Third World Forum, 1997).
21. Ibid.
22. N. Chomsky, "The Passion for Free Markets," *Z Magazine*, Part 1, vol. 10 (May 1997); Part 2, vol. 10 (November 1997).
23. For more information, see http://www.opensecrets.org.
24. S. P. Huntington, "The Clash of Civilizations", *Foreign Affairs*, vol. 72, (Summer 1993): pp. 22–49; S.P. Huntington, *The Clash of Civilizations and the Remaking of World Order* (New York: Touchstone Books, 1996).

25. A. Hochschild, "Let Them Eat War," www.tomdispatch.com (October 2, 2003).
26. R. Kuttner, *The American Prospect* vol. 15 no. 2, February 1, 2004.
27. See, e.g., Wendell Bell, "How Has American Life Changed Since September 11?" Speech given at the Smithsonian's National Museum of American History in Washington, DC, March 9, 2003, published in *Journal of Futures Studies*, vol. 8, no. 1 (August 2003), pp. 73–80.
28. See, e.g., Luciana Bohne, "Learning to be Stupid in a Culture of Cash," http://www.marchforjustice.com/awarenessforum.php.
29. G. Palast, "California and the Power Pirates," from "The Best Democracy Money Can Buy," Znet, (April 23, 2003); and G. Palast, "Arnold Unplugged: It's Hasta la Vista to $9 billion if the Governator is Selected," October 3, 2003. Both on-line at http://www.gregpalast.org.
30. B. Hamm and R. Smandych (eds), *Cultural Imperialism—Essays on the Political Economy of Cultural Domination* (Peterborough: Broadview, 2004).

Part I
The Power Cadres

1

The Bush Family Saga—
Airbrushed out of History

William Bowles

INTRODUCTION

That a family with so many skeletons in its collective closet could
have produced two presidents of the world's most powerful nation
should have every last one of us wondering whether the world has
gone completely mad. Perhaps it has. This may be the lesson we need
to learn from the Bush Family Saga, that far from being an exception
to the rule, it *is* the rule because they and the class and "race" they
represent write the rules. Most important of all is the fact that the
Bush family is not an aberration, but symbolic of the nature of US
imperialism and how it came to be.

The cast is huge and the connections vast and complex. Essentially
though, in tracking the rise of the Bush family, we track the rise of
the American Empire. It is no wonder then that some subscribe to a
conspiratorial view of American history, given all the connections. But
it doesn't require a conspiracy to explain the enormous power that a
handful of families have acquired, merely an understanding of how
the ruling class maintains its power in the United States. One thing is
clear; today's leaders are yesterday's gangsters and the descendants of
the robber barons of turn-of-the-century America. And in a terrible
irony of history, the wealth that built the dominant corporations of
today's America was built with money made from the opium trade
and, as we shall see, the opium trade was instrumental in connecting
the grandfather of the current US president with the rich and powerful
founders of US capitalism—a connection that not only persists to
this day, but one that has been extended into virtually every sector of
US business.

Airbrushed out of history: Prescott Bush—The Nazi's American
Banker

In April 1999, [the then] Texas Governor George W. Bush proclaimed a week of remembrance for the Holocaust. He said, "I urge Texans to never forget the inhumanity of those who perpetrated the Holocaust, and reflect upon our own humanity and our responsibility to respect all peoples."

The ability to continually rewrite history is perhaps the greatest "triumph" of modern capitalism, although it would be more accurate to describe it as "airbrushing out" those events that belie how things came to be. And perhaps the greatest of these "triumphs" is the one performed on the Bush family (although by no means restricted to them), a family that has for the better part of the twentieth century and into the twenty-first, with the able assistance of the corporate media, managed to hide its ignominious past from the public gaze.

In 1823 Samuel Russell founded Russell and Company in order to smuggle opium into China. Russell's head of operations in Canton was Warren Delano Jr, grandfather of Franklin D. Roosevelt, a connection that was to play an important role in the Bush family fortunes, and indeed in the fortunes of the leading industrial corporations such as General Motors, Standard Oil and others, decades later.

Samuel Russell's cousin, William Huntington Russell, founded an alumni association at Yale University in 1832, the Skull & Bones (S&B) alumni, which Prescott Bush, grandfather of the current president, was to join in 1917. Other members include founders of the leading corporations of the time, including Percy Rockefeller (1900) of Standard Oil; Avril Harriman (1913) of Brown Brothers, Harriman banking; Frederick Weyerhauser (1896), paper; three generations of Kelloggs; Alfred Vanderbilt (1899)—a veritable Who's Who of corporate America. Other connected corporations whose founders or corporate bosses attended Yale and belonged to S&B include the founder of Dresser Industries (now part of the Halliburton empire), the Trust Bank of New York, and The Guarantee Bank. Other members of S&B over the past century and more include the key individuals who helped shape US foreign and domestic policy for the entire twentieth century: McGeorge, Hollister, and William Bundy (the Manhattan Project, the CIA, and the Vietnam war respectively); Archibald Coolidge, son of the founder of the United Fruit Company and co-founder of the Council on Foreign Relations; Henry Stimson, Hoover's secretary of state and later secretary of war for both Presidents Roosevelt and Truman; Dean Acheson, chief architect of the Cold War doctrine—the list goes on. In the context of the Bush family, however, from the beginnings of modern corporate capitalism, financial and political links were established between US and German corporations which were to play a central role in the development of international relations for the rest of the twentieth century.[1]

Whilst at Yale, Prescott Bush formed strong friendships with several key people, including Samuel Pryor, owner of the Remington Arms company, and Avril Harriman, whose father, railroad baron E. H. Harriman, gave Avril an investment firm, W. A. Harriman and Company. E. H. hired George Herbert Walker, Prescott Bush's future father-in-law (after whom George Bush Sr is named) the job of running the firm. This set in motion a chain of events that was to continue for the next 90 years.

By 1922 Harriman & Co. was set to expand, and a branch was established in Berlin, where Herbert Walker met Fritz Thyssen, son of the owner of Thyssen and Company, August Thyssen, the main supplier of weapons to the German war machine. Following the crippling postwar settlement, Thyssen was in deep financial trouble. Seeing the writing on the wall, he took steps to protect the family fortune by establishing Bank voor Handel en Scheepvaart in Rotterdam, a bank that was later to play a significant role during and after WWII in protecting the Thyssen family fortunes—with Bush family help.

It has to be remembered that throughout this period German capitalism was "on the rocks," with the German state under threat from a potential socialist revolution. At the end of the war, the country was effectively bankrupt, unemployment was rife, and there were workers' uprisings in Berlin and other cities which were brutally suppressed by the WWI "hero" General Erich Ludendorff, for which the Thyssens and other big capitalists were, of course, eternally grateful. It was through Ludendorff that the Thyssens met Adolf Hitler, who was, according to Ludendorff, "the only man who has any political sense." Fritz Thyssen eventually met Hitler, and the Thyssens, along with other leading industrialists, funded the nascent Nazi Party with its anti-union, anti-communist agenda. However, the party's failed 1923 *coup d'état* resulted in Hitler's imprisonment and (temporary) "fall from grace" with big German capital.

Meanwhile, the meeting between Avril Harriman and Fritz Thyssen resulted in the creation of a US banking operation, jointly owned by Harriman & Co. and the Thyssen family. Set up in 1924, the Union Banking Company (UBC) cemented the economic—and later political—relationship between German and US capital. Occupying the same building as Harriman & Co. at 39 Broadway in New York City, UBC was to become the pivotal connection that led to the relationship between the Bush family and the Nazi Party. It also became the "model" for the relationship that was to emerge in the 1930s between big business under Nazi rule and the mainly pro-Fascist (and anti-Semitic) leaders of the major US corporations.

By the mid-to late 1920s, with the threat of a socialist revolution receding and an economic recovery underway, there were rich pickings to be had by investors, including US businesses, and from which Herbert Walker and Avril Harriman did very well, generating an estimated $50 million for its investors. In 1926 the Thyssen company joined forces with another major industrial family, the Flicks, and formed the United Steel Works (USW). The Flick industrial empire also owned coal and steelworks in Poland. Via the UBC connection, the USW combine brought Herbert Walker on board to manage the new enterprise, and he in turn brought in Prescott Bush to supervise the Thyssen/Flick Polish operations (the Consolidated Silesian Steel Corporation and the Upper Silesian Coal and Steel Company). These two corporations between them owned the bulk of Polish steel and coal production which was to play such a crucial role in the Nazi military machine as well as in the use of slave labor through the Auschwitz concentration camp which was located near the UBC and USW plants.[2]

In 1928, the Nazi Party, strapped for cash and badly in need of funds, approached Fritz Thyssen once again for support, support that Thyssen gave through Bank voor Handel en Scheepvaart, estimated to be around $2 million at today's prices, and in any case enough to finance the purchase and renovation of Hitler's new headquarters, Barlow Palace in Munich.

The 1929 Wall St Crash badly affected the Harriman banking operation and in 1930 Harriman Banking merged with the British bank Brown/Shipley and became Brown Brothers/Shipley. Harriman and Prescott Bush established a new operation, Harriman 15 Corporation, and it was through this new holding company that Prescott Bush came to own stock in USW through its shareholding in Consolidated Silesian Steel Company, with-two thirds owned by Friedrich Flick and the rest by Harriman 15 Corp.

The business/political links established at this time were to last through to the post-WWII period and included not only the UBC/USW connection but also the "commanding" heights of US capital, which embraced Standard Oil, General Motors, the Ford Motor Company, IBM, Alcoa, DuPont, and ITT. All had economic and political relations with German capital, including cross-ownership of industrial plants, not only in Germany but also in what was to become occupied Europe. Indeed, the last thing US capitalism wanted was for the war "to get in the way of doing business," something that has persisted to this day.

The relationship that perhaps best illustrates the connections between US and German capital and the Bush family's hidden role is that of the Consolidated Silesian Steel Corporation and the Upper Silesian Coal and Steel Company and the establishment of the Auschwitz concentration camp close by the coal plants. This was no accident as they were able to draw on a constant supply of slave labor.

Following Hitler's conquest of Europe, Consolidated Silesian Steel was sold outright to Union Banking Corporation and became the Silesian American Corporation managed by Prescott Bush. Its plants continued to supply the Nazi war machine. It was not until 1942 that the US government took action against Union Banking, but Prescott Bush was never prosecuted for "trading with the enemy":

> On October 20, 1942, the US Alien Property Custodian, under the Trading With the Enemy Act, seized the shares of the Union Banking Corporation (UBC), of which Prescott Bush was a director and shareholder. The largest shareholder was E. Roland Harriman. (Bush was also the managing partner of Brown Brothers Harriman, a leading Wall Street investment firm.)
>
> Among the companies financed was the Silesian-American Corporation, which was also managed by Prescott Bush, and by his father-in-law George Herbert Walker, who supplied Dub-a-Ya with his name. The company was vital in supplying coal to the Nazi war industry. It too was seized as a Nazi-front on November 17, 1942. The largest company Bush's UBC helped finance was the German Steel Trust, responsible for between one-third and one-half of Nazi iron and explosives.[3]

What is important to note here is that the Bush/Harriman/Nazi connection was by no means exceptional; the same holds for most of the top US corporations of the period of which the following examples are typical:

> Just after the war erupted in Europe, Standard Oil [now Exxon] sent Frank Howard, a vice-president, to meet Fritz Ringer, a representative of I. G. Farben, at The Hague on September 22, 1939. The two men drew up an agreement, known as the Hague Memorandum, that specified they would remain in business together "whether or not the United States came into the war."[4]

And what held true for Standard Oil also held for the Ford Motor Company:

[Hermann] Goering assured a director of the German Ford subsidiary, Carl Krauch (also with I. G. Farben), that, "I shall see to it that the German Ford Company will not be incorporated into in the Hermann Goering Company ... Thus, we succeeded in keeping the Ford Works working and operating independently of our [the German] government's seizure."[5]

Goering also assured General Motor's president, William Knudsen, in 1933 that "there would be no German annexation of GM's operations in Germany."[6] By the mid-1930s, General Motors were committed to full-scale production of trucks, armored cars, and tanks in Nazi Germany.

Nazi tanks and bombs "settled" this dispute in September, 1939 with the invasion of Poland, beginning World War II. The Nazi army had been equipped by Flick, Harriman, Walker and Bush, with materials essentially stolen from Poland.[7]

Comparable arrangements were made between ITT, DuPont, IBM, and Alcoa and their German subsidiaries which continued to manufacture products and materials vital to the German war machine. In some instances, the supply of critical matériel continued throughout the war, including strategic aircraft lubricants to the Japanese and aluminum to the Germans. None of the leaders of these giant US corporations was ever prosecuted for their role in supplying the German and Japanese war effort. John Loftus, former US Department of Justice Nazi War Crimes prosecutor, had this to say about Prescott Bush and his relationship to the Nazis:

From 1945 until 1949, one of the lengthiest and, it now appears, most futile interrogations of a Nazi war crimes suspect began in the American Zone of Occupied Germany... [The interrogation of] [m]ultibillionaire steel magnate Fritz Thyssen—the man whose steel combine was the cold heart of the Nazi war machine.

They were trying to find out what had happened to Thyssen's billions but without success. Why?

What the Allied investigators never understood was that they were not asking Thyssen the right question. Thyssen did not need any foreign bank accounts because his family secretly owned an entire chain of banks. He did not have to transfer his Nazi assets at the end of World War II, all he had to do was transfer the ownership documents—stocks, bonds, deeds and trusts—from his bank in Berlin through his bank in Holland to his American friends in New York City, Prescott Bush and Herbert Walker. Thyssen's partners in crime were the father and father-in-law of a future President of the United States. ...

The British and American interrogators may have gravely underestimated Thyssen but they nonetheless knew they were being lied to. Their suspicions focused on one Dutch Bank in particular, the Bank voor Handel en Scheepvaart, in Rotterdam.

If the investigators realized that the US intelligence chief in postwar Germany, Allen Dulles, was also the Rotterdam bank's lawyer, they might have asked some very interesting questions. They did not know that Thyssen was Dulles' client as well. Nor did they ever realize that it was Allen Dulles' other client, Baron Kurt von Schroeder, who was the Nazi trustee for the Thyssen companies which now claimed to be owned by the Dutch. The Rotterdam Bank was at the heart of Dulles' cloaking scheme, and he guarded its secrets jealously. ...

The enormous sums of money deposited into the Union Bank prior to 1942 are the best evidence that Prescott Bush knowingly served as a money launderer for the Nazis. Remember that Union Bank's books and accounts were frozen by the US Alien Property Custodian in 1942 and not released back to the Bush family until 1951. At that time, Union Bank shares representing hundreds of millions of dollars' worth of industrial stocks and bonds were unblocked for distribution. Did the Bush family really believe that such enormous sums came from Dutch enterprises? One could sell tulip bulbs and wooden shoes for centuries and not achieve those sums. A fortune this size could only have come from the Thyssen profits made from rearming the Third Reich, and then hidden, first from the Nazi tax auditors, and then from the Allies.[8]

The money, about $1.5 million made from the proceeds of Thyssen's laundered Nazi fortunes, was handed out to Prescott Bush's family, effectively setting them up in business.[9] But most important of all, it was the political and economic connections that they inherited from Prescott, connections that have enabled the Bush family to evolve into a veritable dynasty, a dynasty based on oil and its Middle Eastern/Iranian connections, the "intelligence community" that has its origins in the Vietnam war that extended into the illegal operations conducted by the CIA, including smuggling heroin from the "Golden Triangle," through to the "guns for drugs" operations that were at the core of the Iran/

Contra operations and the US' illegal "low-intensity war" conducted against the Sandinista government of Nicaragua.

The history of the Bush family illustrates something very profound about the nature of capitalism—its opportunistic character hidden beneath the guise of patriotism, democracy, or whatever label is suitable to the occasion. Prescott Bush's links to German Fascism have been mirrored in the post-WWII period by successive US governments and their relationships with dictatorships that, on the one hand, the US government was instrumental in bringing to power and, on the other, by the public pronouncements made about the nature of these dictatorships, most often justified by the "war against communism." A double standard operated throughout these relationships, whether it was with the Shah of Iran, or the innumerable dictatorships of Central and South America, Africa, and the Middle and Far East. George Bush Sr, son of Prescott Bush, personified this relationship as does his son George W. Bush. George Bush Sr was head of the CIA and George Bush Jr had close connections with the Agency. Under their tutelage, the CIA has engaged in the overthrow of governments deemed hostile to US interests and in the furtherance of US strategic interests. The CIA and other organs of the US state have formed relationships with organized crime that involved money laundering, assassinations, and international smuggling operations too numerable to mention here.

THE POSTWAR PERIOD

Prescott Bush's Nazi-based fortunes enabled him to set up George Bush Sr in business—the oil business of course—and it's through these connections in Texas and Oklahoma that George Sr continued along the same trajectory as his father. And once more, the network of connections built over the preceding decades kicked in. One of them was Ray Kravis, who arrived in Texas in 1925 and quickly amassed a fortune made from oil. Kravis also managed the Kennedy family fortunes (made from bootlegging). Prescott lined up a job for George Sr and as a back-up, asked another connection, Henry Neil Mallon, who was president and chairman of the Board of Dresser Industries (now owned by Halliburton), manufacturer of oil well drilling equipment. Dresser had been incorporated in 1905 by Solomon R. Dresser, but had been bought up and reorganized by W. A. Harriman & Company in 1928–29. George Sr however, turned down Kravis's "offer" and went to work for Dresser in Cleveland, Ohio.

Whilst working for Dresser, George Sr met John Overbey, what they call a "landman," someone who identifies potential oil sites and hopefully leases the plot for a pittance and in return for a fee, sells the lease to an oil company, or for a royalty arrangement on any oil discovered. Bush Sr and Overbey established Bush–Overbey and through George's connections the money poured in. By 1953 almost $2 million (a considerable part of which coming from Bush's British connections, including $500,000 from the then director of the Bank of England[10]) had been invested and the company changed its name to Zapata Petroleum. Although the company never made a vast fortune, and for some years reported a loss, the value of Bush's shares rose. In 1954, again utilizing Prescott Bush's connection as a US Senator, Bush and his partners formed Zapata offshore to exploit the newly released offshore mineral rights. Zapata was never a money-making concern, but nevertheless Bush was able to roll over debts and line up more credit. The speculation is that Zapata was a "cover" for US intelligence operations and, given the geographical location of its operations (the Gulf of Mexico and its Cuban connections), and the fact that the company made little or no money, it could still get millions invested into its operations.

BUSH JUNIOR AND BUSH SENIOR—THE CIA YEARS

The current Bush administration is the culmination of a process that has its origins in the post-WWII period and the rise of the Cold War. It also represents the central importance of oil and the related military-industrial complex which, as we have seen, has its roots in the US–German industrial axis formed during the early years of the twentieth century. It is therefore no accident that George Bush Sr was made director of the CIA under the Reagan administration, for he brought with him a range of connections that made him indispensable to Reagan's foreign policy.

The Bush's business network also has connections to the government and the two are interchangeable. From the days of Prescott Bush through to the current president, corporations, private institutions, and government departments have evolved into a network: banking, transportation, oil, weapons, communications, "think tanks," the Department of Defense, the State Department, the White House, the CIA. What is important is the intimate link between business and government, something that goes back to the foundations of modern US capitalism.

To take just one example, Prescott-Harriman-G. W. H. Bush and George Jr, the connections made in the 1930s between Dresser Industries and the Harriman Bank that carried on through Dresser's connections to the "Five Sisters" (the five largest oil companies) and in turn to companies that were later to play a central role in carrying out the Bush doctrine, in which Halliburton and Carlyle were so important. Bush Sr and Bush Jr both had oil companies and not particularly successful ones at that, but what was important were their government connections which enabled them to carry through their policies. In turn, Halliburton bought Dresser, which had already changed hands.

In turn this led to the manner in which private business was greased by oil as the US brokered a deal with the Saudis which gave them military access to the Gulf and Halliburton got $1 billion deal to build Saudi's military and Bush's friends in the oil business did deals with the sheikhs.[11]

It might be said that the Bush presidencies are the culmination of a process that has been a century in the making. For in one way or another, *there's not a single US president in the twentieth century whom the Bush family has not had a direct connection to through one or more relationships.*

The better known associates of the Bush family are those in government, but as presidencies have come and gone, a core group has either remained in the Federal government or moved out into those areas of the corporate world to which they were the closest, then often returning to government, bringing with them even more connections. The process, of course, has been accelerated and transformed by all the mergers and acquisitions that have taken place over the past 20 years. It's why a single company like Halliburton can end up playing such a crucial role in government policy and illustrates what happens to the state when it effectively gets privatized and falls into the hands of a few corporations, ideologues, and vested interests like the military establishment.

Halliburton is actually a collection of already giant corporations that straddle the economic-political bridge and includes oil, its extraction, transport and distribution; and privatized defense, which includes servicing the armed forces, supplies, mercenary forces, training, logistics, communications, and so forth. It has close connections to Carlyle, which is no more than an investment banking concern that "does business" in all the places that Halliburton, Boeing, Grumman *et al.* do. They all sup at the same table—on government contracts.

Collectively, all shared links in the Middle East either through oil (Saudi Arabia) or the CIA in Iran, starting in the 1950s with the overthrow of Mohammed Mossadegh and the installation of Reza Pahlani as the Shah, which in turn came down to oil and the Cold War:

Taking the CIA helm in January 1976, Bush cemented strong relations with the intelligence services of both Saudi Arabia and the Shah of Iran. He worked closely with Kamal Adham, the head of Saudi intelligence, brother-in-law of King Faisal and an early BCCI insider.[12]

BUSINESS CONNECTIONS

The Savings and Loans scandal

In trying to document the innumerable illegal dealings of the various members of the Bush family it's all too easy to provide a simple "list," but what becomes apparent after even the most perfunctory investigation is a network of relationships that unites the past 40 or so years of Bush family involvement in a series of events, with each piece in the jigsaw linked by one thing: US foreign and domestic policy and business interests. To quote Gary W. Potter of Eastern Kentucky University:

> To some, the savings and loan (S&L) scandal of the 1980s is "the greatest ... scandal in U.S. history" (Thomas, 1991: 30). To others, it is the single greatest case of fraud in the history of crime (*Seattle Times*, June 11, 1991). Some see it as the natural result of the ethos of greed promulgated by the Reagan administration (Simon and Eitzen, 1993: 50). To others, it was a conspiracy to move covert funds out of the country for the CIA (Bainerman, 1992: 275).
>
> S&Ls were living, breathing organisms that fused criminal corporations, organized crime and the CIA into a single entity that served the interests of America's political and economic elite.[13]

A number of S&Ls including First National Bank, Palmer National Bank, Indian Springs Bank, Vision Banc Savings, Sunshine State Bank, were used to funnel money as part of the illegal funding of the Nicaraguan Contras, funding that was paid for through the sale of cocaine and involved the CIA "asset" Manuel Noriega, former strongman of Panama, now languishing in solitary confinement in a US federal prison, and the Colombian drug cartels.[14] Jeb Bush, second son of George Bush Sr, was the one of the connections

> to Miami Contras and right-wing anti-Castro Cuban-Americans. In the mid-1980s, he took contributions to the Miami Republican Party from Leonel Martinez who was arrested in 1989 and later convicted of bringing 300 kilos of cocaine into the U.S.

Jeb was also connected to the drug money laundering scandal of the CIA-linked the Bank of Credit and Commerce International, in 1986–1987.

In the mid-1980s, Jeb worked for businessman Miguel Recarey, Jr. whose mafia links went back 20 years. During the 1980s, Recarey is thought to have embezzled $100 million from Medicare through his Miami-based company, International Medical Centers, which also treated wounded Contras at its Florida hospital.

When the Bush administration bailed out Broward Federal S & L in 1988, for $285 million in bad loans, Jeb and partner Armando Cordina (leader of the right-wing Cuban American Foundation) didn't have to repay their $ 4.1 million loan.

Jeb successfully lobbied Dad in 1990 for the release from jail of Orlando Bosch, who fired a bazooka at a Polish freighter in the Miami harbour in 1968 and master-minded the explosion of a Cuban airliner killing 73 people over Barbados in 1976.[15]

And so, too, with Neil Bush, third son of George Bush Sr:

Between 1985 and 1988, Neil was also a director of Silverado Banking Savings and Loan in Denver, Colorado. Silverado lent over $200 million to Good and Walters. Neil did not disclose his connections to Good and Walters, when—as a Silverado director—he voted to grant them the loan. Good raised Bush's JNB salary from $75,000 to $125,000 and gave him a $22,500 bonus. In total, Bush received $550,000 in salaries from Walters and Good. Neil also received a $100,000 loan from Good that was later forgiven.

In 1990, Federal regulators filed a $200-million lawsuit against Neil and other officers of Silverado Banking. Regulators determined that Neil was completely dependent on Good and Walters for his income. An expert hired by regulators said Neil suffered from an "ethical disability."

In 1990, Neil was reprimanded by the U.S. Office of Thrift Supervision for "multiple conflicts of interest" and ordered to pay $50,000. Neil's $250,000 legal bill was paid by a legal defense fund formed by Thomas Ashley, a friend of Neil's father.[16]

Ignite!

This may be small fry by comparison with all the other Bush clan scams, but nevertheless Ignite!Learning has made Neil Bush $20 million over the past three years, largely through a contract with Florida State Education Authority, where his brother Jeb is governor.[17] Not bad for a guy who ran Silverado S&L into the ground. With accusations of nepotism flying around, especially now that Neil is trying to get the Florida school system to buy into his learning software (at $30 a pop per student per year), it's no wonder. Connected is the wholesale privatization of state services, which opens such areas as education to the predations of people like Neil Bush and indeed, the whole issue of influence peddling and nepotism.

Yet the S&L scandal, which cost the US taxpayer an estimated $3 trillion, was merely one facet of an international network needed to move vast sums of money around the world and involved the biggest crash in banking history, the Bank of Credit and Commerce International (BCCI), which is still the object of legal actions. BCCI was the de facto CIA bank for laundering the billions of dollars needed to mount its international operations.

The Bank of Credit and Commerce International

The mosaic of BCCI connections surrounding Harken Energy may prove nothing more than how ubiquitous the rogue bank's ties were … But the number of BCCI-connected people who had dealings with Harken—all since George W. Bush came on board—likewise raises the question of whether they mask an effort to cozy up to a presidential son.[18]

George Bush Sr's position as head of the CIA under Reagan and his connections to oil, the anti-Castro Cubans, the Nicaraguan Contras and the Iran hostage crisis of 1979 had a common element: BCCI. BCCI was the bank of choice for the CIA and the innumerable "proprietaries" that the CIA operated which included airlines (e.g. Air America) and an unknown number of front companies utilized for illegal arms deals, spying, and mercenary operations spanning the planet, but that have their genesis in the Vietnam war where, following the defeat of the French at the hands of the Viet Minh, found the US, via the CIA, taking over the drug smuggling operations initiated by the French intelligence services.[19]

The BCCI saga is still on-going. Suffice it to say that aside from illegal money-laundering deals that revolved around drugs for guns, the other major use of BCCI (as well as the Nugan Hand and Banco Nazionale Del Lavoro (BNL) or the Vatican Bank, both of which were also used for moving CIA and drug money) was the financing of a variety of illegal operations that required "plausible deniability" on the part of the US government.

The BCCI–Bush connection is, it could be argued, an "accidental" one, but it's highly unlikely even if it is difficult to track. Nevertheless the seeds are all there, including George Sr's CIA connection (as head of it) in the 1970s and the links to BCCI as well as his long association with James R. Bath, an investor in Arbusto. Bath, a Houston businessman and old friend, was also an investor in BCCI (and on the board of BCCI). BCCI was a convenient "channel" for moving money to fund the various illegal enterprises being undertaken at the time, including Iran/Contra, the Iranian arms sales, CIA money-laundering operations, connections to powerful Middle Eastern businessmen, the Vatican and its right-wing connections through BNL:

> BCCI defrauded depositors of $10 billion in the '80s in what has been called the "largest bank fraud in world financial history" by former Manhattan District Attorney Robert Morgenthau.[20]

Perhaps this extract from Texas Connections gives you an idea of the reach:

> Sheikh Abdullah Bahksh of Saudi Arabia, a 16% shareholder in Harken Energy at the time, was represented by a Palestinian-born Chicago investor named Talat Othman, who served with George W. Bush on the board of Harken Energy. Othman made at least three separate visits to the White House to discuss Middle East affairs with then President George Bush. At about the same time, and just prior to the Gulf War, Harken Energy, with no previous international or offshore drilling experience, was awarded a 35-year petroleum exploration contract with the emirate of Bahrain.
>
> Sheikh Bahksh emerged as a co-investor in the Bank of Commerce and Credit International (BCCI), a criminal enterprise since dissolved, that existed primarily as a mechanism for obtaining political influence using Middle Eastern oil money. Bahrain's prime minister, Sheik Khalifah bin-Sulman al-Khalifah, was a major investor in BCCI's parent company, BCCI Holdings, of Luxembourg. Through its commodities affiliate, Capcom, BCCI was used as a money laundering service by drug traffickers, arms dealers, etc. BCCI's front man in the U.S., and the person chiefly responsible for its takeover of First American Bank in the U.S., was Kamal Adham. Adham is referred to in the Kerry Committee report on BCCI as having been "the CIA's principal liaison for the entire Middle East from the mid-1960's through 1979." He was also the head of intelligence for Saudi Arabia during the time George Bush Sr. was Director of the CIA.[21]

Arbusto Oil, the Carlyle Group and the bin Laden Connection

Oh what a tangled web we weave. Salem bin Laden, one of 57 children their father Mohammed sired with his twelve wives, and Bush were founders of the Arbusto Energy oil company in Texas. Salem bin Laden— like his father—died in a plane crash but not before the Arbusto Energy Oil Company, founded in 1978, had become hugely successful. Later, Spectrum 7 Corp bought out Arbusto (now called Bush Exploration Co.). In 1986, with the company on the verge of bankruptcy, it was purchased by Harken, and even though Bush Exploration Co. had debts of $3 million, Harken paid Bush $2 million for his stock.

Time magazine described Bath in 1991 as "a deal broker whose alleged associations run from the CIA to a major shareholder and director of the Bank of Credit & Commerce." BCCI, as it was more commonly known, closed its doors in July 1991 amid charges of multi-billion-dollar fraud and global news reports that the financial institution had been heavily involved in drug money laundering, arms brokering, covert intelligence work, bribery of government officials and—here's the kicker—aid to terrorists.[22]

There are so many connections between the Bushes, the "defense" establishment and the global trade in arms that the mind boggles. That it barely gets a mention in the mainstream media (except, of course, occasionally simply to "report" it) is a scandal of the grandest proportions. But it only goes to show the power of big business and the political class they have installed in both the US and the UK (after all, John Major former British prime minister is employed by the Carlyle Group, and BAE Systems, the major arms supplier to the UK, is part-owned by Carlyle). Not only do the connections beggar belief, but the sheer hypocrisy of the Bush government should put it in a new category in the *Guinness Book of Records*. The Bush family tentacles extend to many of the armed conflicts going on in the world. There's no business like war business!

THE CARLYLE GROUP AND GOVERNMENT: A REVOLVING DOOR RELATIONSHIP

On the morning of September 11, 2001, Frank Carlucci (Reagan's secretary of defense), former secretary of state James Baker III, and representatives of the bin Laden family were attending a board meeting of the Carlyle Group at the Ritz-Carlton in Washington, DC.

The Caryle Group is a private equity corporation with some $12–14 billion in assets. Aside from being the nation's eleventh largest defense contractor and a force in global telecommunications, it has investors in major banks and insurance companies, billion-dollar pension funds and wealthy investors from Abu Dhabi to Singapore. It also owns health care companies, real estate, internet companies, a bottling company, and *Le Figaro*, the French newspaper. There are five central players in the "revolving door" between business and government: George Bush Sr and George Jr, Secretary of Defense Donald Rumsfeld, James Baker III, Vice President Dick Cheney and Frank Carlucci:

> "Carlyle is as deeply wired into the current administration as they can possibly be," said Charles Lewis, executive director of the Center for Public Integrity, a nonprofit public interest group based in Washington. "George Bush is getting money from private interests that have business before the government, while his son is president. And, in a really peculiar way, George W. Bush could, some day, benefit financially from his own administration's decisions, through his father's investments. The average American doesn't know that and, to me, that's a jaw-dropper."[23]

The Bush–Carlyle connection also has less well-known links that are connected directly to the current "war on terror", including major investments in South Korea, which include KorAm Bank and telecommunication's company Mercury.

But it is the bin Laden–Saudi connection that attracts the most interest. A Carlyle-owned company trains the Saudi Arabian National Guard. Carlyle also advises the Saudi royal family on the Economic Offset Program, designed to encourage foreign investment in Saudi Arabia. And after the 9/11 attacks, reports surfaced of Carlyle's involvement with the Saudi bin Laden Group, the $5 billion construction business run by Osama's half-brother, Bakr. The bin Laden family invested $2 million in the Carlyle Partners II fund, which includes in its portfolio United Defense and other defense and aerospace companies. Following 9/11, the bin Laden Group purportedly severed its connection with Carlyle, but Carlyle continues to maintain its many and diverse business relationships with Saudi Arabia.

Corporations such as Carlyle have really come into their own with the wholesale privatization of government under Bush Jr based on the connections that extend back to the 1980s and earlier, of which Carlyle is the best known but by no means the only result of two decades of "neoliberal" economic policy. Carlyle personifies the symbiotic relationship between politics and business with the Bush family as well as the connection with those in the various branches of government who decide on policy and who are also connected to the Bushes. These include Richard Perle, the "Prince of Darkness," who in turn sits on the boards of major corporations, including Hollinger International, the giant media corporation. Perle, one of a handful of influential "neo-con advisors" to the current Bush administration with strong connections to the Israeli right wing, is yet another facet of Bush's Middle East strategy.

Enron connection

The Bush–Enron connection started in 1988 when George Bush Jr first met Kenneth Lay, former chairman of Enron. Bush Jr lobbied the Argentine government on behalf of Enron for a multi-million dollar gas pipeline deal, which had already been rejected by the government of Raul Alfonsin. The pipeline was approved by the succeeding administration of President Carlos Saul Menem, leader of the Peronist Party and a friend of President Bush Sr:

> George W. was an active player in his father's 1988 election campaign, which was also heavily funded by Lay, Enron and Enron executives. George H. W. Bush's campaign finance chairman Robert Mosbacher, who worked intimately with the younger Bush, became an Enron board member in December 1987, more than a year before the elder Bush became president and eight years before W. made Lay's acquaintance.[24]

Enron was Bush Jr's single biggest campaign contributor, with over three-quarters of a million dollars over an eight-year period, including donations for Bush Jr's campaign for the Texas governorship. Moreover, over half of Bush's major campaign contributors had links to Enron, including Morgan-Stanley (banking and originally a Prescott Bush connection, though then known by another name). Other companies are Anderson Consulting, Crédit Suisse, First Boston, Citigroup's Salomon Smith Barney, and Bank of America.[25]

Neil Bush also performed services on behalf of Enron, in his case in Kuwait. In 2002 when the Enron bubble burst, the Bush administration claimed that it did nothing to assist the company but the facts belie this:

> [Bush's] Treasury Secretary O'Neill was aware of Enron's impending collapse and did nothing to warn or protect the stockholders. A

man so intimate with Wall Street, and with Kenneth Lay, could not have missed the disparity between Enron's stock value and the dire financial news he was getting from Enron's chairman. Rather than perform the duties of his office and step in to protect the thousands of Americans who would lose their life savings within the capital market that deserved and expected his guidance, O'Neill chose only to inform Mr. Bush and then remain silent. This was a dire breach of the clearly stated requirements of his position, one that cost a lot of people a lot of money.[26]

Moreover, the Bush administration did everything in its power to stave off the impending collapse, with Bush personally intervening to stop caps on the soaring price of electricity in California (brought about by Enron's manipulation of the supply of electricity). In addition, Bush granted Kenneth Lay broad influence over the administration's energy policies, including the choice of key regulators to oversee Enron's businesses.[27]

Enron and Bush personify the era of "funny money," that is, profits based on currency speculation, asset-swapping, buy-outs, the "dot com" boom (and subsequent bust) of course and, most importantly, the drive to deregulate the energy industry, once more highlighting the symbiosis between business and government policies—policies that guaranteed billions of dollars in profits at the expense of the public in what amounts to grand larceny and which has left the US with the biggest national debt in its history and many of the states on the verge of bankruptcy.

International Medical Centers: The Jeb Bush connection

Miguel Recarey's International Medical Centers faced pressure in 1985 to comply with the "50–50" rule, which prohibits certain HMOs from having more than half of its customers on Medicare. According to Recarey, the middle son of then-Vice President Bush called Health and Human Services Secretary Margaret Heckler (meanwhile, IMC paid Bush's company a $75,000 "real-estate consultant" fee). Former HHS [Health & Human Services] chief of staff McClain Haddow says Bush's call gave IMC a waiver to the 50–50 rule, and Recarey allegedly bilked $200 million in Medicare funds while leaving 150,000 seniors without coverage. Jeb Bush, the GOP loser in Florida's 1994 governor's race, denies calling Heckler.[28]

This is a murky story with connections to the Nicaraguan Contras, the Mafia, Cuban-American terrorists, Iran/Contra, bribery and corruption, cover-ups, and the CIA. Essentially, IMC was contracted to give medical assistance to the Nicaraguan Contras, but the story is in fact a lot more complex and gives you some idea of just how interconnected events really are when you're dealing with the Bush clan:

Cuban exile Miguel Recarey, who ... earlier assisted the CIA in attempts to assassinate President Castro.

Recarey ... employed Jeb Bush as a real estate consultant and paid him a $75,000 fee for finding the company a new location, although the move never took place, which raised questions at the time. Jeb Bush did, however, lobby the Reagan/Bush administration vigorously and successfully on behalf of Recarey and IMC. "I want to be very wealthy," Jeb Bush told the *Miami News* when questioned during that period.

In 1985, Jeb Bush acted as a conduit on behalf of supporters of the Nicaraguan contras with his father, then the vice-president, and helped arrange for IMC to provide free medical treatment for the contras.

Recarey was later charged with massive Medicare fraud but fled the US before his trial and is now a fugitive.

Most controversially, at the request of Jeb, Mr Bush Sr intervened to release the convicted Cuban terrorist Orlando Bosch from prison and then granted him US residency.

According to the Justice Department in George Bush Sr's administration, Bosch had participated in more than 30 terrorist acts. He was convicted of firing a rocket into a Polish ship which was on passage to Cuba. He was also implicated in the 1976 blowing-up of a Cubana plane flying to Havana from Venezuela in which all 73 civilians on board were killed.[29]

The Bush–Cuban connection is central to an understanding of the later involvement with the Nicaraguan Contras, for both involved organized crime and the use of mercenary armies. In Cuba it was the protection of gambling and prostitution (in the pre-Castro days), and with the Contras it was the drugs that paid for the illegal supply of weapons to the Nicaraguan Contras.[30] Both connections proved useful, the first in the attempts to overthrow the Castro government, the second, to remove the Sandinistas. In both instances, it meant breaking the law in order to pursue a foreign policy. The IMC proved to be a useful front, one of many used by the CIA.

In Florida, Jeb Bush (then head of the Dade County Republican Party) operated as the Republican administration's unofficial link with

Cuban exiles, the Contras and Nicaraguan exiles in Miami. During this period, Jeb also aligned with Leonel Martinez, a Miami-based, right-wing Cuban-American drug trafficker associated with Contra dissident Eden Pastora (who was later assassinated by an alleged CIA operative based in Costa Rica). Jeb forged business ties with Contra supporter Miguel Recarey, a right-wing Cuban and major contributor to PACs controlled by then Vice President George Bush Sr.[31]

The network extends in many directions, but with the Bush family at the center of the web. The common links are: the CIA, drugs, anti-Castro Cubans, money-laundering operations, gun-running and a plethora of "front" organizations, many of which are still in operation today but now operating in the "war on terror."

MARVIN BUSH AND THE KUWAITI CONNECTION

Marvin P. Bush, brother of President Bush Jr, is the founder (1993) and managing partner of a private investment company, Winston Partners Group of Vienna, Virginia. He is also the managing general partner of Winston Growth Fund, LLP, Winston International Growth Fund, LP, and Winston Small Cap Growth Fund, LP—all related companies.

Before this, he spent twelve years in the investment business with the firms of Mosley, Hallgarten, Estabrook and Weeden, Shearson Lehman Brothers, and John Stewart Darrel & Company.

In January 1998, Marvin was appointed to the Board of Directors of the Fresh Del Monte Produce company, the giant fruit company that makes the canned goods we buy in our supermarkets. Del Monte is owned by a very wealthy family from Kuwait, the Abu-Ghazaleh family. Mohammed Abu-Ghazaleh is the CEO and he has several family members on the Board alongside Marvin. Another member of the Fresh Del Monte Board of Directors is Stephen Way, a major Bush fundraiser. Way is the head of the Houston-based HCC Insurance Holdings Company. In early 2000, Way arranged the appointment of Marvin Bush to the Board of Directors of HCC. In that transaction, Marvin secured not only a very large salary, but also a sweet stock option deal.[32]

HCC was one of the insurers of the World Trade Center and the major investor in HCC is Kuam Corporation. Marvin was also named to the Board of Directors of the Stratesec Company, another large, publicly traded firm that handled security for the World Trade Center. Virginia-based Stratesec is a provider of high-tech security systems. Two of the other major customers for which they provide security are Dulles International Airport in Washington, DC and the Los Alamos

National Laboratory. Stratesec's revenues recently went up by 60 per cent, due to what the company describes as "new customers." Prominent people at Stratesec include former Reagan operatives Barry McDaniel and General James A. Abrahamson (who was involved in the Reagan Star Wars project). Stratesec is a company heavily interrelated with the Kuwam Corporation ("Kuw" = Kuwait; "am" = America; Kuwam is a major Kuwaiti company involved in many activities, including the aircraft business; and it also owns Fresh del Monte). Stratesec's chief executive is also the managing director of Kuwam Corporation and Kuwam's chairman, Mishal Yousef Saud Al Sabah, sits on Stratesec's Board of Directors.

What is apparent from this tangle of relationships is the sheer scale of the Bush family business connections; perhaps even more revealing is the fact that they have taken almost a century to "mature" to the point where they now constitute a mafia of global proportions, which sits at the center of power, aided by the increasing concentration of ownership of key sectors of the global economy with which the Bushes have direct and indirect connections. These connections have become all too apparent as the "War on Terror" has replaced the "Red Menace" as the central rationale for US capitalism's strategy, personified in the curtailing of civil liberties and the construction of a global security state, all under the guise of the "War on Terror."

GEORGE BUSH AND THE CONSTRUCTION OF THE GLOBAL SECURITY STATE

George Bush Sr as Ronald Reagan's vice president presided over the culmination of the decades-long war on communism, whose apogee was its support of those fighting the Soviet occupation of Afghanistan. It is here that we find the political and business connections of the Bush clan coming into their own. It is also here that we find all the connections with oil, weapons, the media, covert operations, and the ultra right-wing Reagan players finding a voice for a program three decades in the making.

9/11 was the pivot, and here once more the Bush clan, aided by the 'neo-con' cabal now firmly ensconced at the center of power, had all the right weapons at its disposal, best expressed through H.R. 3162, or The Uniting and Strengthening America by Providing Appropriate Tools Required to Intercept and Obstruct Terrorism Act, or USA Patriot. And yet again, Bush's corporate connections were instrumental in the making of this key piece of legislation, for through it, the political elite were able to consolidate their grip on power and call upon the corporate forces needed to implement the construction of Mussolini's vision of a corporate state; anti-union, anti-working class and, above all, where the interests of the corporation are installed at the center of political power through the privatization of the public sphere.

The state now has all the weapons it needs to suppress domestic dissent and the necessary corporate connections to carry it out.

ChoicePoint

ChoicePoint was the firm that Katherine Harris, Florida's Secretary of State during the 2000 elections, paid to erase 57,000 names from the voter rolls which made the difference between a Bush and a Gore presidency.[33]

> ChoicePoint is a database company with prominent Republicans on its board and payroll, and it now offers up over 20 billion pieces of information on American citizens to law enforcement and intelligence agencies. Since passage of the USA Patriot Act, the feds can access all that formerly private info without a search warrant.[34]

However, the connection between ChoicePoint, the Patriot Act, and the Bush family is more complex. Enter two corporations: Winston Partners and Sybase. Sybase developed 'Patriot-compliant' software and a major shareholder in Sybase is Winston Partners, part of the Chatterjee Group. One of Winston's co-owners is Marvin Bush.

ChoicePoint "compliant"

> SEC filings show that Winston Partners LP owns 1,036,075 shares in Sybase; Winston Partners LDC holds 1,317,825 shares; and Winston Partners LLC owns 1,221,837 shares. The shares owned by the subsidiaries are collectively managed in funds for Winston Partners by Pernendu Chatterjee. ...
> The company is also a significant government contractor ... with contracts from the Agriculture Department, the Navy ($2.9 million in 2001), the Army ($1.8 million in 2001), the Defense Department ($5.3 million in 2001), Commerce, Treasury and the General Services Administration among others. The federal procurement database lists Sybase's total awards for 2001 as $14,754,000.
> Sybase is only one of the companies with federal contracts from which Marvin Bush's firm derives financial benefit. Winston Partners' portfolio also includes Amsec Corp., which got Navy contracts worth $37,722,000 in 2001.[35]

Also on the board of ChoicePoint is Richard Armitage, deputy secretary of state, president of Armitage Associates, international lobbying, marketing, and strategic planning consulting firm who was investigated for his role in the Reagan era Iran/Contra scandal.[36] What goes around, comes around ...

Once more, the vested interests of corporations that are intimately connected to the Bush family are intrinsic to the domestic and foreign policy objectives of the Bush administration. Sybase software is part of the ChoicePoint system, which is part of the Patriot Act, which is part of the whole damn system for keeping track of everybody and everything we do, read, visit, buy, and no doubt think about. At every step of the way, Bush family members are making money out of the "war on terrorism." Never before have the interests of government and business been so closely aligned, indeed they are in lock-step with one another.

CONCLUSION: A CORPORATE *COUP D'ÉTAT*

The assault on the rights of citizens, won at great cost and over generations of struggle, has, since the 1970s, been steadily eroded to the point that we are now left with a façade of the original, a cardboard mock-up that has all the appearances of democracy, civil rights, and so forth, but with virtually no substance.

Central to this de facto corporate *coup d'état* is the Bush family and its business and political network which this essay has only scratched the surface of. What is clear is that big business is now firmly ensconced at the center of government. No longer is there any pretense of government representing the people. The transformation wrought by the Bush dynasty is perhaps best summed up with the following quote:

> The Cheney–Bush pirates are about to birth a new brood of billionaire pillagers and parasites *with no direct connection to the well being of the domestic economy* and those of us who depend on it.[37]

NOTES

1. Kris Milligan (ed.), *Fleshing out Skull & Bones* (n.p.Trineday, 2003).
2. Ibid.
3. Richard N. Draheim, *The Bush Nazi Connection (The Draheim Report)* (Texas: Dallas Libertarian Post, 2000).
4. John Spritzler, *The People as Enemy* (Montreal: Black Rose Books, 2003) pp. 89–90.
5. Ibid., p. 92.

6. Ibid., p. 94. Not only did William Knudsen advocate appeasement with Hitler, GM's vice president, Graeme K. Howard, praised Hitler and advocated appeasement with the Nazis in his book *America and the New World Order* (New York: Scribner, 1940).

7. The Prescott Bush-Nazi connections are extensively documented in Webster G. Tarpley and Anton Chaitkin, *George Bush: The Unauthorized Biography*, much of which is to be found in Milligan, *Fleshing out Skull & Bones*. Office of Alien Property Custodian, Vesting Order No. 248. The order was signed by Leo T. Crowley, Alien Property Custodian, executed October 20, 1942; F.R. Doc. 42–11568; Filed, November 6, 1942, 11:31 a.m.; 7 Fed. Reg. 9097 (November 7, 1942). See also the *New York City Directory of Directors* (available at the Library of Congress). The volumes for the 1930s and 1940s list Prescott Bush as a director of Union Banking Corporation for the years 1934 through 1943. Alien Property Custodian Vesting Order No. 259: Seamless Steel Equipment Corporation; Vesting Order No. 261: Holland-American Trading Corp. Alien Property Custodian Vesting Order No. 370: Silesian-American Corp. The *New York Times*, on December 16, 1944, ran a five-paragraph, p. 25 article on the actions of the New York State Banking Department. Only the last sentence refers to the Nazi bank, as follows: "The Union Banking Corporation, 39 Broadway, New York, has received authority to change its principal place of business to 120 Broadway." Fritz Thyssen, *I Paid Hitler* (1941; reprinted Port Washington, NY: Kennikat Press, 1972), p. 133. Thyssen says his contributions began with 100,000 marks given in October 1923, for Hitler's attempted *putsch* against the constitutional government. Confidential memorandum from US embassy, Berlin, to the US Secretary of State, April 20, 1932, on microfilm in *Confidential Reports of U.S. State Dept., 1930s, Germany*, at major US libraries. October 5, 1942, Memorandum to the Executive Committee of the Office of Alien Property Custodian, stamped CONFIDENTIAL, from the Division of Investigation and Research, Homer Jones, Chief. Now declassified in United States National Archives, Suitland, Maryland annex. See Record Group 131, Alien Property Custodian, investigative reports, in file box relating to Vesting Order No. 248. *Elimination of German Resources for War*: Hearings before a Subcommittee of the Committee on Military Affairs, United States Senate, Seventy-Ninth Congress; Part 5, Testimony of [the United States] Treasury Department, July 2, 1945. p. 507: Table of *Vereinigte Stahlwerke* output, figures are a percentage of the German total as of 1938; Thyssen organization, including Union Banking Corporation pp. 727–31. See also Interrogation of Fritz Thyssen, EF/Me/1 of September 4, 1945 in US Control Council records, photostat on p. 167 in Anthony Sutton, *An Introduction to The Order* (Billings, Mt: Liberty House Press, 1986). *Nazi Conspiracy and Aggression—Supplement B*, by the Office of United States Chief of Counsel for Prosecution of Axis Criminality, United States Government Printing Office (Washington, 1948), pp. 1597, 1686. See also William L. Shirer, *The Rise and Fall of the Third Reich* (New York: Simon and Schuster, 1960), p. 144. *Nazi Conspiracy and Aggression—Supplement B*, p. 1688.

8. Ibid.

9. Milligan, *Fleshing out Skull & Bones*, pp. 276–9.

10. *George Bush: The Life of a Lone Star Yankee* (New York: Scribner, 1997).

11. Craig Unger, *House of Bush, House of Saud: The Secret Relationship Between the World's Two Most Powerful Dynasties* (New York: Scribner, 2004).

12. Kevin Phillips, "The Barrelling Bushes," *Los Angeles Times*, January 11, 2004.

13. Gary W. Potter, "1980s, USA: Money Laundering for Contras, the Mob and the CIA," Eastern Kentucky University. (http://www.ncf.ca/coat/our_magazine/

links/issue43/articles/mone_laundering_for_contras.htm). See also *Covert Action Information Bulletin*, Summer 1992; and Stephen Pizzo, Mary Fricker and Paul Muolo, *Inside Job: The Looting of America's Savings and Loan* (New York: McGraw-Hill, 1989); *Los Angeles Times* (July 31, 1990), p. 1; Jonathan Kwitny, "How Bush's Pals Broke the Banks," *The Village Voice* (October 20, 1992), p. 27.
14. See note 21.
15. Jack Colhoun, "The Family That Preys Together," *Covert Action Information Bulletin*, no. 41 (Summer 1992).
16. Ibid.
17. Greg Palast, *The Best Democracy Money Can Buy* (London: Constable and Robinson, 2003).
18. *Wall Street Journal* (December 6, 1991), p. A4.
19. Jonathon Kwitney, *The Crimes of Patriots: A True Tale of Dope, Dirty Money, and the CIA* (New York: Touchstone Books; reprint edition September 1988).
20. Wayne Madsen, "Questionable Ties: Tracking bin Laden's Money Flow Leads Back to Midland, Texas," *In These Times* (November 12, 2001).
21. "The BCCI Affair." A Report to the Committee on Foreign Relations, United States Senate, by Senator John Kerry and Senator Hank Brown. December 1992 (102d Congress 2d Session Senate Print 102–140), http://www.fas.org/irp/congress/1992_rpt/bcci/.
22. James Hatfield, *Fortunate Son* (New York: Soft Skull Press, 2003).
23. Leslie Wayne, "The Carlyle Group Elder Bush in Big G.O.P. Cast Toiling for Top Equity Firm," *New York Times* (March 5, 2001).
24. "The Enron Corporation" http://www.enron.com/corp/; Tony Clarke, "Enron: Washington's Number One Behind-the-Scenes GATS Negotiator," Special to CorpWatch (October 25, 2001), http://www.corpwatch.org/issues/wto/featured/2001/tclarke.html; John Hoefle, "Bush Crew and Enron: Conflict Of Interest and Reality," http://www.differentvoices.com/article1037.html; *Channel 4 News Special Reports.* "Power Failure (India)," Reporter: Jonathan Rugman, June 21, 2000 http://www.channel4.com/news/home/20010621/Story07.htm; "Enron Failure may be Biggest," by Luisa Beltran, CNN, November 29, 2001; http://europe.cnn.com/2001/BUSINESS/11/29/enron/index.html; "Enron Fights for Life after Bid Collapse," BBC, November 29, 2001; http://news.bbc.co.uk/hi/english/business/newsid_1681000/1681522.stm; "The Enron Corporation. Corporate Complicity in Human Rights Violations (India)," http://www.hrw.org/reports/1999/enron/enron-toc.htm.
25. Huck Gutman, "Bush's Biggest Donors Had Links to Enron," *Common Dreams* (February 15, 2002).
26. William Rivers Pitt, "Enron, Bush Officials Face Serious Legal Questions," *Truthout* (January 15, 2002).
27. See note 22.
28. "Fugitive Fingers Jeb Bush," *Mother Jones* (July/August 1995).
29. Duncan Campbell, "The Bush Dynasty and the Cuban Criminals," *Guardian* (December 2, 2002).
30. Lawrence E. Walsh, Final Report of the Independent Counsel for Iran/Contra Matters. Volume III: Comments and Materials Submitted by Individuals and Their Attorneys Responding to Volume I of the Final Report (Washington DC: U.S. Government Printing Office, December 3, 1993), 1150 pp.
31. See *Covert Action Information Bulletin* (Summer 1992).

32. Margie Burns, "Bush-Linked Company Handled Security for the WTC, Dulles and United," *Prince George's Journal* (Maryland) (February 4, 2003).
33. Palast, *The Best Democracy Money Can Buy* (London: Constable and Robinson, 2003).
34. "Dirty Dealings in Data," *Jim Hightower's Lowdown* (Saturday, April 5, 2003).
35. Margie Burns, "Marvin Bush Cashes In On Gvt. Security." http://www.americaheldhostile.com/ed112802–1.shtml (November 28, 2002).
36. See note 27.
37. "Rule of the Pirates: The $200 billion payday," *BlackCommentator* (December 5, 2002), http://www.blackcommentator.com/19_commentary_pr.html.

2

War Hawks and the Ugly American: The Origins of Bush's Central Asia and Middle East Policy

Andrew Austin

Joined by British military forces, the United States invaded the Central Asian country of Afghanistan on October 7, 2001. In what was tagged "Operation Enduring Freedom," the US overthrew the ruling clique, the Taliban, and destroyed training camps of the terrorist organization al Qaeda, located in the mountains of Tora Bora. The US emplaced an interim government led by Hamid Karzai, a weapons financier for anti-Soviet mujahedeen and associate of the US Central Intelligence Agency (CIA).

On March 17, 2003, again in concert with British forces, the US military invaded Iraq. "Operation Iraqi Freedom" resulted in the overthrow of Saddam Hussein and the ruling Ba'ath Party. The US formed an interim national government, the Iraqi Governing Council, led by Ahmad Chalabi, a US-educated banker, prominent member of the London-based Iraqi National Congress, CIA associate, and a protégé of high-ranking Pentagon officials. The Council dissolved on June 1, 2004. Dr. Iyad Allawi, co-founder of the CIA-sponsored Iraqi National Accord, was appointed as prime minister of the interim government.

The financial cost of these undertakings has been staggering. On September 7, 2003, President Bush asked Congress for $87 billion to cover the costs of operations in Central Asia and the Middle East. This was in addition to $79 billion Congress had already budgeted for the military campaigns. War and reconstruction expenditures overseas would come against the backdrop of the largest federal budget deficit in US history ($412.5 billion in 2004), a national economy mired in a "jobless recovery," and 36 million Americans living in poverty. Despite this, Congress approved Bush's request less than two months later.

In human terms, the Bush wars have been nothing short of tragic. Marc Herold, a professor at the University of New Hampshire, estimates civilian deaths in Afghanistan to be 3,767 as of December 2001. Afghan fighters and friendly fire have killed several dozen US troops and injured many more. In September 2004, the number of US soldiers killed in Iraq surpassed 1,000, representing the highest number of casualties in any US-involved conflict since the Vietnam war. The official number of US soldiers wounded in Iraq comes to 7,532 as of September 27, 2004.[1] How many Iraqi military personnel US and British forces have killed or injured is unknown, but observers suspect it is in the thousands. As of October 18, 2004, the independent organization Iraq Body Count estimates civilian casualties from "Operation Iraqi Freedom" to be between 13,278 and 15,357.

From a review of public opinion surveys, the majority of Americans believe that the threat of Islamic terrorists and rogue states warrants these great financial and human costs. So frightened by the specters of terrorism and dictatorship are the Americans that they apparently have forgotten that Bush promised them during the second debate with Democratic presidential candidate Al Gore that he would not make the United States the "ugly American" by engaging in "nation-building." However, it seems likely, or at least one hopes this is the case, that majority belief will be hard to maintain in the face of overwhelming evidence that suggests, to the contrary, that the Bush regime and its allies, principally Great Britain, orchestrated the war for purposes other than national security and making the world a more peaceful place. This chapter discusses other possible reasons for Bush's wars, and details major players and ideologies shaping US foreign policy in the current geopolitical context.

A NATIONAL SECURITY STRATEGY?

The Bush administration justified the invasion of Afghanistan on the grounds that the terrorist organization believed to have masterminded the attacks on the United States on September, 11, al Qaeda, led by Saudi millionaire Osama bin Laden, enjoyed the protection of the Taliban. The government defended its invasion of Iraq based upon two claims: Iraq possessed weapons of mass destruction and the Ba'ath Party had links with al Qaeda.

The principled basis for intervention was set out in the September 2002 White House report, *The National Security Strategy of the United States of America*. This document detailed a pre-emptive strike policy appealing to the principle of anticipatory self-defense. The policy of pre-emption represents a dramatic departure from America's previous defense posture. Historically, a grave and imminent danger to national security triggered the right to self-defense. However, while a justifiable anticipatory self-defensive action must indicate a credible and imminent threat to national security, pre-emptive self-defense need indicate only a potential or probable eventuality. Under this more expansive definition of what constitutes legitimate self-defense, mere official belief that a nation desires to acquire weapons of mass destruction is enough to justify the use of force. As the document averred, "We cannot let our enemies strike first."

The authors of the report, led by National Security Advisor (NSA) Condoleezza Rice, characterized the new defense philosophy as "a distinctly American internationalism." The report pledges the use of military force to encourage "free and open societies," to fight for American ideals and values, especially private property, and to win the "battle for the future of the Muslim world." Policy-makers tied the doctrine of pre-emption to imperatives of regime change and nation-building in a "post 9/11 world." A solution to the alleged problems "rogue states" present for national security is the possibility the government may have to overthrow an existing government unilaterally.

However, in the current world order, the law on the use of armed force, the *jus ad bellum*, prohibits discretionary and unilateral military force and tightly constrains the use of reactive force of arms to self-defense or a collective decision by the UN community to prevent unlawful aggression. Moreover, any retaliatory action by a country must be proportional, and it is a recognized principle in international law that while self-defense is a legitimate response while under attack, it is not legitimate *post facto*—that is, once an attack has ended, self-defense is prohibited.

Bush's rationale for invading Afghanistan based on the September 11, 2001 attack is deeply problematic with respect to *jus ad bellum*. Harboring terrorists may have made the Taliban complicit in the criminal behavior of al Qaeda, but such behavior is insufficient for determining direct responsibility necessary to warrant retaliatory military action. The administration never adequately explained why destruction of government buildings, infrastructure, towns and villages, resulting in the deaths of thousands of civilians, was necessary to apprehend bin Laden and dismantle al Qaeda. That the US promised the UN "surgical strikes" against Taliban targets to minimize "collateral damage" (military jargon for harming civilians) does not negate Bush's tragic moral lapse and his flouting of international law. In any case, targeting was poor, targets were wrongly identified, bombing was often indiscriminate, and the weapons used, such as cluster bombs, led to numerous civilian casualties. Military action has so far failed to bring bin Laden and many of his top operatives to justice. This is in part because Bush diverted resources in the hunt for al Qaeda terrorists to pursue war in Iraq, as former special assistant to Bush, Richard Clarke, has pointed out.[2]

The justification for launching an invasion of Iraq to overthrow the Ba'ath government was equally problematic. The policy of regime change is, from the point of view of the White House, a corollary to pre-emptive self-defense. If a state is pursuing weapons of mass destruction and delivery systems capable of threatening America at some distant, albeit uncertain future point, then a pre-emptive self-defensive action would be regarded as a means of preventing this eventuality. However, while instances of anticipatory self-defense are numerous in history, historical instances of pre-emptive self-defense are not (the most notable case was the 1981 Israeli attack on the Osirak nuclear reactor outside of Baghdad). Moreover, it is widely regarded as necessary for the international community, operating through the UN, to consent to the use of pre-emptive force. International law prohibits unilateralism in pre-emptive self-defensive action. Therefore, Bush was obliged to secure UN sanction for a military strike against Baghdad. The US, joined by a small number of other countries, defied the consensus of the international community and invaded Iraq without UN authorization.

Even if we set aside international law, evidentiary reasons given for pre-emptive action in Iraq were insufficient, incomplete, and, in many cases, fabricated. Authorities have found neither weapons of mass destruction nor effective delivery systems in Iraq. And, whatever the case may be, credible evidence for WMDs would have had to exist *before* military action was taken. The consensus of the international intelligence community is that Saddam destroyed such weapons at the conclusion of the US–Iraq war in 1991. And any claim the US invaded Iraq in retaliation for 9/11, however illegitimate according to international law, had no evidentiary basis. The administration admitted during a meeting with congressional leaders on September 17, 2003 that it never had evidence connecting Saddam to 9/11.

If the Bush administration's reasons for plunging two countries into confusion and chaos seem irrational, it is only because one has failed to grasp the real reasons behind the warmongering. These are the ulterior motives for going to war: control of the gas and oil supplies in two regions and reshaping power in the Middle East with an eye to creating conditions for a resolution to the Israeli–Palestinian conflict. The material and political interests driving White House policy are held together by the president's religious ideology, an apocalyptic strain of Christianity known as Christian Zionism, and sold to the public via deft propaganda designed by Bush's principal political advisor, Karl Rove.

GAS AND OIL

No understanding of Bush's foreign policy ambitions is adequate without a grasp of the central importance of America's dependency on fossil fuels. The chief sources of energy are petroleum (30 per cent), natural gas (24 per cent), and coal (23 per cent). North Americans consume over 21 million barrels of oil a day, more than any other region in the world.[3] Domestic oil and gas production cannot meet public demand. Given this situation, securing cheap and readily available sources of fossil fuels is an imperative for an administration beholden to gas and oil companies (many Bush administration officials are major players in the fossil fuels industry).

Outside of the Middle East, the Caspian Sea region (the "Stans," including Azerbaijan, Kazakhstan, Turkmenistan and Uzbekistan) contains the largest proven natural gas and oil reserves in the world. Central Asia has almost 40 per cent of the world's gas reserves and 6 per cent of its oil reserves. The US has long desired not only to secure these reserves for its increasing energy appetite, but also to control transport,[4] which permits command over prices and undermines the hegemony of the Organization of the Petroleum Exporting Countries (OPEC). US interest in Central Asia became transparent with the withdrawal of the Russian military from Afghanistan in 1989 and the collapse of the Soviet system in 1991. By 1992, mostly US-based companies (Amoco, ARCO, British Petroleum, Exxon-Mobil, Pennzoil, Phillips, TexacoChevron, and Unocal) controlled half of all gas and oil investments in the Caspian region.[5]

The details are revealing. Within less than five years of the fall of the Soviet Union, Unocal, in association with Delta Oil (Saudi Arabia), Gazprom (Russia), and Turkmenrozgas (Turkey), began negotiating with various Afghan factions to secure the right to construct a trans-Afghan pipeline. Unocal worked closely with the Taliban to "educate them about the benefits such a pipeline would bring this desperately poor and war-torn country," according to a company statement. However, Unocal withdrew from the consortium in December 1998 citing "sharply deteriorating political conditions in the region" and the reluctance of the US and the UN to recognize the Taliban as the legitimate government of Afghanistan.[6] Then, in the spring of 2002, after the US toppled the Taliban regime and installed a puppet government, oil companies and the interim ruler, Hamid Karzai, along with Mohammad Alim

Razim, minister for mines and industries, reopened the pipeline project talks. Razim has stated that Unocal was the frontrunner to obtain contracts to construct the pipeline with funds from the reconstruction of Afghanistan (funds supplied by the US taxpayer). Crucial to these negotiations is the US envoy to Kabul, Afghanistan-born Zalmay Khalilzad. As special envoy, he ostensibly reports to Secretary of State Colin Powell. However, as a National Security Council (NSC) official and special assistant to the president for Southwest Asia, Near East and North Africa, he reports directly to NSC chief (and former board member of TexacoChevron), Condoleezza Rice. Khalilzad has a long history working in Republican governments.[7] He has also served as a lobbyist for the Taliban. In August 1998, after al Qaeda allegedly bombed the US embassies in Kenya and Tanzania, Khalilzad presented in a widely read article what would become key elements of the Bush policy on Afghanistan. His contention was that administration officials under Clinton in 1994 and 1995 underestimated the danger the Taliban "posed to regional stability and US interests." He predicted that Afghanistan's importance would grow "as Central Asia's oil and gas reserves, which are estimated to rival those of the North Sea, begin to play a major role in the world energy market." Afghanistan, properly managed, would serve as a "corridor for this energy,"[8] the men of big oil noted, along with Khalilzad Afghanistan's relevance. Through the mechanism of "Operation Enduring Freedom," they have established a political economic presence in Central Asia.

The second largest proven oil reserves in the world are in Iraq (only Saudi Arabia has larger reserves). In 1978, Saddam Hussein, then vice chairman of Iraq, boasted, "One of the last two barrels produced in the world must come from Iraq." As late as spring 2002, the US was obtaining 800,000 barrels a day from Iraq, making that country the sixth most important source of oil for North American consumption. As Bush rattled sabers over its differences with the regime of Saddam Hussein, petroleum companies switched to other suppliers, cutting Iraq exports by some 70 per cent. However, US petroleum companies anticipated that oil would flow again after tensions subsided and UN sanctions were concluded, thus lowering oil prices again. And reducing oil prices was an imperative. Crude oil had risen from a low of $10 a barrel in 1997 to $30 a barrel in 2000. Projections indicated prices would remain at that level without a change in the structure of the world oil markets. The possibility of a massive and cheap source of fossil fuel drew the interest of other countries, as well. Russian, European, and Chinese companies negotiated or were negotiating contracts with Saddam's regime in the run-up to war.[9]

Unfortunately for these other countries, the US under Bush had scheduled Saddam Hussein for elimination. By overthrowing the Ba'ath Party, the Bush regime nullified the contracts negotiated by other countries. As former CIA directory James Woolsey put it, "If [these other countries] throw in their lot with Saddam, it will be difficult to the point of impossible to persuade the new Iraqi government to work with them."[10] Faisal Qaraghoil, the director of the London office of the INC, maintained the new Iraqi government would not be bound by any previously negotiated contracts. And INC leader Ahmed Chalabi stated that a US-led consortium would develop Iraq's oil fields. From the standpoint of US energy interests, the war was necessary to establish US control over Iraqi oil and to stabilize world oil prices.

WOLFOWITZ AND PERLE: ARIK'S AMERICAN FRONT

The Jerusalem Post has frankly and aptly described the neo-conservatives at the core of policy-making in the Bush White House as "Arik's American Front."[11] Paul Wolfowitz and Richard Perle are identified in particular as principal members of Ariel Sharon's organization in Washington. Hence the focus of this section will be on these two officials.

Wolfowitz has a long history of public service in the United States. He served as deputy assistant secretary of defense for regional programs from 1977 to 1980 under Jimmy Carter. He was head of the State Department's Policy Planning Staff from 1981 to 1982 under Ronald Reagan, where he played a major role in shaping Reagan's Cold War strategy. From 1989 to 1993, he served as under secretary of defense for policy under George Bush Sr. Wolfowitz is currently deputy secretary of defense under Bush Jr. A Pentagon special unit, the Office of Special Plans (OSP), headed by Wolfowitz, developed much of the initial information that found its way into Powell's controversial testimony given before the UN Security Council on February 5, 2003. Wolfowitz organized OSP to counter doubts about the CIA's Iraqi intelligence.

In 2002, Wolfowitz received the Henry M. "Scoop" Jackson Distinguished Service Award from the Jewish Institute for National Security Affairs (JINSA). Senator Jackson was the Democrat's pre-eminent hawk in the 1970s and early 1980s. So dedicated was he to the military industrial complex that his colleagues nicknamed him the "Senator from Boeing." Jackson's understanding of Israel's war against the Palestinians shaped his foreign policy thinking. In 1979, at the Conference on International Terrorism, sponsored by the Jonathan Institute, Jackson characterized terrorism as "a modern form of warfare against liberal democracies." The goal of this warfare, he said, "is to destroy the very fabric of democracy." Jackson praised Israel's suppression of Palestinian terrorists: "In providing for her own defense against terrorism, Israeli courage has inspired those who love freedom around the world." He rejected the premise that the targets of terrorism should negotiate with terrorists. Referring to the ambitions of the PLO, Jackson said, "To insist that free nations negotiate with terrorist organizations can only strengthen the latter and weaken the former." He also rejected the premise of Palestinian statehood: "To crown with statehood a movement based on terrorism," he said, "would devastate the moral authority that rightly lies behind the effort of free states everywhere to combat terrorism."

During the 1970s, Jackson and his supporters and aides became increasingly disillusioned with the Democratic Party. The Democrats had moved away from confrontation with terrorism, seeking instead to defuse the source of the conflict they believed spawned terrorists. According to the hawks, this "blame America first" approach inevitably meant laying responsibility for terrorism at the feet of those states that had become the terrorists' targets, since it forced the public to consider the possibility that terrorism was a reaction by oppressed people to colonialism and imperialism. This shift in the party forced many of Jackson's aides, including Elliot Abrams, Douglas Feith, Frank Gaffney, Jeane Kirkpatrick, and, most importantly, Wolfowitz and Perle, to switch to the Republican side, obtaining offices in the Reagan and Bush administrations.

Wolfowitz used the JINSA awards ceremony as an opportunity to show that Bush was following in the footsteps of Jackson, a hero of Israeli hardliners. Describing Bush as a leader "determined to move forward strategically, pragmatic step after pragmatic step toward a goal that the faint hearted deride as visionary," Wolfowitz said Jackson "would have been proud and pleased to know our President." Admonishing media characterizations of Bush's inner circle as "hawks" by noting that Jackson rejected the label ("I just don't want my country to be a pigeon," Jackson once remarked), Wolfowitz condemned appeasement. "Freedom cannot be defended, much less advanced by the fainthearted who shun all risks," said Wolfowitz. "And it cannot be advanced if we believe that evil dictators can be brought around to peaceful ways without at least the threat of force."

Wolfowitz's desire to shift American foreign policy towards a more aggressive imperialism is well over a decade old. When, in 1992, Secretary of Defense Dick Cheney requested versions of the Defense Planning Guidance (DPG) directive from Colin Powell, the chairman of the Joint Chiefs of Staff, and from Wolfowitz, then under secretary of defense for policy, the grandeur of Wolfowitz's thinking contained in his version of the document captivated the defense secretary. In his DPG, Wolfowitz was critical of the way Bush Sr had handled the 1991 Iraq war. He believed the continuing presence of Saddam Hussein clearly indicated Bush had ended the war prematurely. Wolfowitz proposed that the US militarily intervene in Iraq to guarantee the US access to raw materials, especially oil, and to remove the threats of terrorism and weapons of mass destruction. Wolfowitz argued that "with the demise of the Soviet Union, American doctrine should be to assure that no new superpower arose to rival the US' enlightened domination of the world." To achieve this goal, Wolfowitz "called for pre-emptive attacks and ad hoc coalitions." Moreover, the US must be prepared to go it alone when "collective action cannot be orchestrated." [12]

Although Bush Sr went along with Powell's more pragmatic plan in 1992, Cheney and Wolfowitz believed they were on the verge of realizing their dream of *Pax Americana* in a second Bush term. However, a long and deep economic downturn erased Bush's wartime popularity. To their dismay, the electorate selected Arkansas governor Bill Clinton for president in 1992 and the neo-conservatives were ousted from power. Not content with waiting for the next Republican administration, Wolfowitz and several other intellectuals formed the Project for a New American Century (PNAC), a think tank "to make the case and rally support for American global leadership." Top corporate, military, and political figures aligned themselves with PNAC, including Elliot Abrams (Reagan State Department), Dick Cheney, Frank Gaffney (president of the Center for Security Policy), William Kristol (Dan Quayle's chief of staff and editor of the conservative publication *Weekly Standard*), and Donald Rumsfeld. Powerful economic interests threw their support behind PNAC.[13]

PNAC emerged in 1997 wielding a document calling for the US to "take its place in history as the dominant global force and achieve greatness by being bold and purposeful." PNAC asked in its statement of principles, "Does the US have the resolve to shape a new century favorable to American principles and interests?" This PNAC intellectuals doubted. "We seem to have forgotten the essential elements of the Reagan administration's success," they lamented. Those successful elements were a "military that is strong and ready to meet both present and future challenges; a foreign policy that boldly and purposefully promotes American principles abroad; and national leadership that accepts the US' global responsibilities."

In an open letter to President Clinton, dated February 19, 1998, Wolfowitz, Perle, Feith, and Wurmser, joined by Rumsfeld, Abrams,

Kristol, John Bolton (current under secretary for international security), Frank Carlucci (Reagan defense secretary), Richard Armitage (current deputy secretary of state), and others, made the argument that "Saddam must be overpowered." The letter asserted that the "danger" imposed by Saddam, "cannot be eliminated as long as objective is simply 'containment,' and the means of achieving it are limited to sanctions and exhortations." They urged the White House to "provide the leadership necessary to save ourselves and the world from the scourge of Saddam and the weapons of mass destruction that he refuses to relinquish."

In 2000, PNAC released the report *Rebuilding America's Defenses*. This document would become the blueprint for Bush's *National Security Strategy* discussed above. According to this earlier document, America "has for decades sought to play a more permanent role in the Gulf regional security. While the unresolved conflict with Iraq provides the immediate justification, the need for a substantial American force presence in the Gulf transcends the issue of the regime of Saddam Hussein." Subduing the region required more stable launching points into the various countries. Saudi Arabia had become, PNAC argued, problematic as a staging area because of its "domestic sensibilities." Moreover, after removing Saddam from power, "Iran may well prove as large a threat."

The judicial *coup* of 2000 that led to the Bush presidency provided the opening the neo-conservatives had been waiting for: an ideological president receptive to their ideas. PNAC had positioned them well for the takeover of US foreign policy. The administration appointed Wolfowitz to his current post. Under the direction of Rumsfeld, the Pentagon created the Defense Policy Board (DPB), an ostensibly informal working group composed of former government officials and military experts serving as an advisory body to the Pentagon on defense issues, put Richard Perle in charge, and plugged the PNAC directly into executive power.[14] Not taking a second Bush term for granted, Wolfowitz, according to *Time* magazine, pressed the White House to go to war with Iraq immediately after the terrorist attacks on the World Trade Center and the Pentagon.[15] He would have to wait until after the invasion of Afghanistan, but, in the end, he got what he had for so long desired: the overthrow of Saddam Hussein, the occupation of Iraq, and the removal of US military bases from Saudi Arabia.

In 2002, *The Jerusalem Post*, reflecting on Wolfowitz's JINSA Distinguished Service Award, singled out Wolfowitz as "one of the principal architects of the US war against Islamic terrorism" a war hawk who "comes from a pedigree of successful strategists schooled by Henry Jackson." The neo-conservatives "acknowledge realistically that as the land of freedom and liberty, the US is locked in a constant and never-ending struggle against movements and ideologies that would murder innocents and blot out freedom." And where did they acquire such realism?

> As their teacher, Henry Jackson made clear, the inspiration for much of what they stand for comes from watching and emulating Israel. It is the legacy of the Jewish state, indeed of the Jewish people as the solitary fighter combating terrorism against innocent civilians that captivated these men's attention thirty years ago. It was Israel's struggle that made them recognize that terrorism, like Communism—the major threat of that day—must be fought without compromise.[16]

Thirty years lurking in the shadows, Perle, tagged by comrades and enemies alike as the "Prince of Darkness," has been at the forefront of foreign policy thinking about the Middle East. Like Wolfowitz, Perle was among those Jackson devotees who hitched their political career to the conservative Republican wagon, serving as assistant secretary of defense for international security policy from 1981 to 1987 under Reagan. During the 1980s, Perle criticized the Reagan and Bush administrations for their support of Saddam during the Iraq–Iran war in the 1980s; and, as early as 1991, he advocated overthrowing the regime of Saddam Hussein. Until recently, he was chairman of the DPB.[17] Additionally, he has served in non-governmental elite organizations, such as the Council on Foreign Relations (CFR), the American Enterprise Institute (AEI), and JINSA.

Perle pursues his aggressive Middle East vision by working for countries on both sides of the Atlantic. In 1996, while serving with the prominent Israeli think tank, The Institute for Advanced Strategic and Political Studies (IASPS), Perle, along with Douglas Feith, the current under secretary of defense for the US, and David Wurmser, current special assistant in the State Department, authored the report *A Clean Break: A New Strategy for Securing the Realm*, for the Likud Party, Israel's leading right-wing party. The document advised then prime minister, Benjamin Netanyahu, to walk away from the Oslo Accord. In 1997, in *A Strategy for Israel*, Feith followed up on the *Clean Break* report and argued that Israel should reoccupy the areas under the control of the Palestinian Authority. "The price in blood would be high," Feith wrote, but such a move would be a necessary "detoxification" of the situation. This was, in his view, "the only way out of Oslo's web." In the report, Feith linked Israel's rejection of the peace process to the neo-conservatives' obsession with the rule of Saddam

Hussein and the Ba'ath regime. "Removing Saddam from power," Feith wrote, is "an important Israeli strategic objective."

With Wolfowitz, Perle advised the White House to jettison the previous administration's theory that reducing Jewish–Muslim antagonism would garner support for an attack on Iraq. They advocated targeting regimes aiding and abetting terrorism in a unilateral fashion. They linked Saddam with terrorist groups operating in Palestine, claiming, "as long as Saddam is in power, terrorists will have a place to hide."[18] A major US paper reported that Perle told the administration to "give Sharon full support" in his suppression of Palestine. "We need to bring the maximum pressure to bear on Arafat, not Israel," Perle said.[19] (Support for the Sharon approach was, therefore, a *cause* in the Bush policy shift towards Iraq, not a result of it.)

For their part, Sharon and his advisors aggressively lobbied Washington to expand the definition of terrorism to include groups and states bent on Israel's destruction. In meetings Bush and Sharon "shared their mutual concerns about the threats posed by terrorism and the development of advanced weapons by Iraq and Iran."[20] This tactic was clever, the Israeli press noted at the time, for it gave Bush the room he needed to pursue his Middle East policy while maintaining an ostensive "hands-off" policy on the Israel–Palestinian conflict. The strategy allowed for the manipulation of liberals who would aid in the perception that Bush was disengaged by complaining about disengagement. Couched in this fashion, Sharon's message "could lead to victory for the Wolfowitz camp," wrote the *Jerusalem Post*.[21]

With a green light from Washington, Israel has not only intensified operations in Palestinian territory, but has also stepped up hostilities towards Lebanon and Syria. This is what the neo-conservatives had hoped for. As early as December 2001, Perle called on Israel to bomb the Bekaa Valley and the Hamas headquarters in Damascus. By the US stepping back from Israel, Sharon could not only take Arafat out, but could also enlarge the conflict. Indeed, Sharon came into office with a well-conceived strategy for thwarting the Middle East peace process. This was not initially apparent to US observers who saw Sharon's pre-election belligerence as the acts of a crude anti-Palestinian bigot. But Sharon had in fact created the conditions to justify heightened levels of repression in the occupied territories by visiting Jerusalem's al-Aqsa mosque at the Temple Mount. This controversial action sparked the second Intifada, unleashing intense violence lasting for years. The Israel government would pull out of the peace process and launch a massive military campaign against Palestinians under this pretext. What was viewed at the time as an act of ignorance and intolerance was in fact a brilliant strategic move by a hardline right-winger bent on erasing the Oslo blunder.

In 2002, Frances Fitzgerald noted that "for years before the Bush administration took office Rumsfeld and Wolfowitz were calling for [Saddam's] overthrow on the grounds that he posed a danger to the region, and in particular to Israel."[22] FitzGerald cites a panel discussion at the Washington Institute in June 1999 where Wolfowitz clarified his views about the connection between Iraq and the peace process. He believed George Sr's invasion of Iraq averted a nuclear war between Iraq and Israel and that "Yasser Arafat was forced to make peace once radical alternatives like Iraq had disappeared." Wolfowitz continued, "The US needs to accelerate Saddam's demise if it truly wants to help the peace process." Perle has likewise been clear on this connection: "We shouldn't wait," he said. "We should go after Iraq." Why? "The removal of Saddam would be a tremendous step forward for the peace process. We need to take decisive action, and when we do and are successful, it will greatly strengthen our ability to do other things in the region."[23]

At an AIPAC conference held in the spring of 2002, "America and Israel Standing Together Against Terrorism," attended by half of the US Senate and 90 members of the US House of Representatives, former Israeli Prime Minister Benyamin Netanyahu said, "There has never been a greater friend of Israel in the White House than President George W. Bush." The conference saluted 13 senior administration officials. Talking points AIPAC officials handed out to delegates echoed Sharon's message that he is "waging his part of the war on terrorism."[24] The talking points stated, among other things, that the US and Israel "are victims of well-organized and well-funded extremist organizations" and "Israel must defend against this terror just as surely as the US must fight and destroy al Qaeda and other terrorist groups with global reach."

In the final analysis, President Bush and his team of advisors have successfully reversed the Clinton peace strategy. The new Middle East policy shifts the emphasis towards the problems of the Palestinian Authority. This has required Bush and the State Department to distance themselves from the peace process and support Sharon's refusal to negotiate with the Palestinians in an environment of heightened conflict. At every opportunity, Sharon has made a point of reiterating his position: he will never deal with Palestinians under fire. During their meetings, Bush and Sharon have agreed that, until the violence subsides, negotiations cannot begin. Sharon has done his part to make sure violence does not wane, assassinating prominent Palestinians such as Hamas spiritual leader Sheikh Ahmed Yassin.

GOD'S MAN OF THE HOUR

What moves Bush to support these policies? The oil interests are, perhaps, obvious. But why would an evangelical Christian from Crawford, Texas find compelling the neo-conservative desire to entrench the power of the Israeli state? Opposition to the Oslo approach to Middle East peace reflects a particular brand of Judeo-Christian belief, Christian Zionism, of which Bush is a devotee. Christian Zionists believe that Israel must be restored to its biblical boundaries before Christ can return to collect the souls of believers.

Bush shares this view with numerous congressional Republicans. Led by House Majority Leader Tom Delay of Texas, evangelical Christians in Congress have contended that Washington must allow Israel to fulfill biblical prophecy. Senator James Inhofe has said, from the floor of the Senate, "The Bible says that Abram removed his tent, and came and dwelt in the plain of Mamre, which is in Hebron, and built there an altar before the Lord." "Hebron is in the West Bank," the Senator from Oklahoma emphasized. "It is at this place where God appeared to Abram and said, 'I am giving you this land.'" Inhofe then drew this startling conclusion: "This is not a political battle at all. It is a contest over whether or not the word of God is true."[25]

Also at the core of Christian Zionism is the belief that God endorses the American way of life. In his 2002 State of the Union address, Bush declared, "The liberty we prize is not America's gift to the world; it is God's gift to humanity." In Bush's view, no country is excused from accepting the heavenly present of "democratic capitalism." "Events aren't moved by blind change and chance," Bush stated at the 2003 National Prayer Breakfast; rather, "the hand of a just and faithful God" determines all circumstances. Bush assured Americans they can "be confident in the ways of Providence, even when they are far from our understanding." History, according to Bush, is the unfolding of God's will. "Behind all of life and all of history, there's a dedication and purpose." It is in the context of a worldview that rests upon Providence that members of the Bush administration have interpreted recent events as celestial signs God has ordained Bush to lead America through the final hour of His divine plan.

Members of the Bush administration see the attacks on the World Trade Center and the Pentagon as signs that God selected Bush to lead a crusade against evil. Insiders have revealed that war planners bring their strategies and tactics to the president where he and members of his administration pray over their vision and translate the text into articles of faith. According to Julian Borger, "While most people saw the extraordinary circumstances of the 2000 election as a fluke, Bush and his closest supporters saw it as yet another sign he was chosen to lead. Later, September 11 'revealed' what he was there for."[26] After his speech to Congress on September 20, 2001, Bush received a telephone call from speechwriter Mike Gerson, who said, "Mr. President, when I saw you on television, I thought—God wanted you there."[27] Tim Goeglein, deputy director of the White House public liaison, remarked to a religious reporter, "I think President Bush is God's man at this hour." Ralph Reed, former director of the Christian Coalition, said God chose George Bush to be president because "He knew George Bush had the ability to lead in this compelling way." Religious leader Gary Bauer once remarked, "A man of God is in the White House." *Time* has reported, "Privately, Bush even talked of being chosen by the grace of God." When he was Texas governor, Bush called Fort Worth televangelist James Robison and said, "I've heard the call. I believe God wants me to run for president."[28]

David Frum, the speechwriter who coined the phrase "axis of evil," exposed the depth of fundamentalism in the Bush administration in his book *The Right Man*. According to Frum, Bush and his advisors strive to create in each of their targets an enemy comparable to Reagan's Evil Empire, a construct steeped in religious metaphor. During the writing of the 2002 State of the Union address, Gerson came to Frum and challenged him to "sum up in a sentence or two our best case for going after Iraq." Frum came up with the phrase "axis of hatred," which he felt "described the ominous but ill-defined links between Iraq and terrorism." Gerson substituted the word "evil" for "hatred" because it made the slogan sound more "theological." According to Frum, in an interview with Julian Borger, "It was the sort of language President Bush used."[29]

GENERAL ROVE

A computer disk was found in Lafayette Park containing this advice from Bush principal advisor Karl Rove to his colleagues: "Focus on War." When the Republican Party met in Austin, Texas in the winter of 2002, Rove told the devoted there to exploit the war in Afghanistan for political gain. Revelations of Rove's marching orders confirm what critical observers have understood for a long time: Rove is the architect of the political side of the war strategy. Although the White House has endeavored to give the appearance of distancing Rove from foreign policy advising, desiring to portray him as playing no role in military decisions, he is still referred to as "General Rove." Karl Rove is well aware of the perception among Americans that Republicans are stronger on national defense issues, and hammers the theme of Republican military prowess to the party faithful.

Rove has become deeply involved in Bush's Middle East policy. When the White House considered pressuring Congress to back away from voting on a resolution in support of Israel, Rove convinced the White House not to do so. Rove is out front pushing the president's rhetoric of Sharon as a "man of peace." Fearful conservative Christians and Jews in the Republican Party were becoming disillusioned with Bush's stance on the Israeli–Palestinian conflict, believed to be largely due to Powell's disturbing concern with forging peace between the two peoples, Rove sent Wolfowitz to speak at a high-profile rally in support of Israel in April 2002.[30]

Rove is the principal architect of the Bush image. He runs the three main propaganda offices in the White House: the Office of Political Affairs, which runs polls and focus groups to develop strategies for shaping messages; the Office of Public Liaison, which promotes Bush priorities through outreach to constituencies and public interest groups; and the Office of Strategic Initiatives, which coordinates the planning and implementation of the overarching strategy for achieving Bush's plans. It was Rove who picked Ellis Island, with the Statue of Liberty glowing in the background, as the site where Bush delivered his September 11 address to the nation. It was Rove who orchestrated the president's "Top Gun" landing on the aircraft carrier with the banner heralding the end of the war in Iraq: "Mission Accomplished." It was Rove who claimed Bush's disappearance in the aftermath of 9/11 was because Air Force One was under attack. Rove timed the debate over Iraq in the fall of 2002 to benefit the Republicans by distracting the electorate from Bush's dismal domestic record.

In one of the White House's more audacious propaganda efforts, a film was released on the cable television network Showtime, *DC 9/11*, depicting Bush not as the man who sat unconcerned before schoolchildren after being told the South Tower had been hit by a jet airliner, or as a confused president who was whisked away to an underground bunker in Nebraska for a crash course in how to act presidential in a military crisis, but rather as a take-charge cowboy: "If some tinhorn terrorist wants me, tell him to come and get me," actor Timothy Bottoms, who plays Bush in the movie, thunders; "I'll be at home. Waiting for the bastard." A secret service agent says, "But Mister President—," but is cut off by Bush: "Try 'Commander-in-Chief' whose present command is: Take the President home!" *DC 9/11* was written and produced by Lionel Chetwynd, a close associate of Bush, who worked with Rove to develop the "documentary." Chetwynd, the founder of the Wednesday Morning Club, an organization of Hollywood conservatives organizing support for Bush, is a member of the White House Committee on the Arts and Humanities.

REGIME CHANGE AND THE UGLY AMERICAN

Regime change has become the central tenet in Bush's foreign policy as an aggressive doctrine of intervention has taken shape. The president has dedicated himself to materializing the doctrine of the "ugly American" he condemned at the Wake Forest University debate in October 2000. The Bush doctrine contains three basic principles, as outlined by PNAC:

- The US shall develop the capacity to strike in a preemptive manner any country it deems as a threat. Bush argued in the 2002 State of the Union address that just as America's "enemies view the entire world as a battlefield," so must the US.
- The US shall actively pursue regime change. Americans must dedicate themselves to the task of nation building. Countries targeted for intervention are "rogue states" and their "terrorist allies" that are "arming to threaten the peace of the world."
- The US shall promote liberal democratic principles around the world. In a 30 January 2003 memorandum to opinion leaders, PNAC wrote, "Because the US has a 'greater objective'—a greater purpose—in the world, Bush sees in the war not just danger but an opportunity to spread American political principles, especially into the Muslim world."

America's shift towards a renewed imperialism is the work of Scoop Jackson's protégés. Since the fall of the Soviet Union, members of the DPB–PNAC clique have believed they are entitled to a political moment comparable to 1949, when elite arrangements—the NSC, Bretton Woods, and NATO—shaped the post-WWII world.[31] The invasion and occupation of Iraq has been for years the central element in their polyarchic designs. If the US can force Iraq to become a "democratic beacon" in the region, the neo-cons theorize, then other Middle Eastern countries will follow, touching off a "democratic tsunami." Democracies in Syria, Iran, and other countries in the Middle East will diffuse anti-American anger and create a context leading to a resolution of the Israeli-Palestinian conflict, ushering in a new age of peace and liberal economic development in the region. However, the doctrine of the pre-emptive strike is the ideological cover over the practice of conducting foreign policy via military means. Linking a people to "global terrorism" and manufacturing evidence of "weapons of mass destruction" are tactics that can be used to demonize any country that exists as an obstacle to national interest. Now that the US is the world's only superpower, Washington feels more confident in deploying military means to conduct foreign affairs.

Why are Americans behind this president and his policies? Certainly the degree of religiosity expressed by Americans in public opinion surveys explains much of it. Polls show that around 40 per cent of Americans describe themselves as born-again or evangelical Christians. Among born-again Christians, Bush's popularity remains high. In the battle between Christianity and Islam, the Jews occupy a central position between them. Many Christians today believe Jesus had to die to fulfill God's plan for the Earth and that the Jews must have a homeland before Christ can return. The rise of this brand of fundamentalist Christianity almost certainly lies behind much of America's support of Bush. The faithful are likely to agree with the president and his advisors that he has been chosen by God to protect Israel and to repel Islam.

Another reason for popular support for Bush's policies is found in the ignorance of Americans concerning basic facts about the official enemy. Nearly half of all Americans believe Saddam Hussein was part of the terrorist network that attacked the US on September 11, 2001. In a poll conducted by Steve Kull, an analyst for the Program on International Policy Attitudes (University of Maryland), one third of Americans believe US forces actually found WMDs and 22 per cent believe Saddam *used* biological and chemical weapons in the latest conflict. In fact, no WMDs have been found or were used. Half of all Americans believed Iraqis were among the 19 hijackers. Another survey found only 17 per cent of respondents knew no hijackers were Iraqi. In fact, none of the hijackers was Iraqi.

But at the root of Americans' collective willingness to fall so readily for the administration's propaganda is an overwhelming sense of fear and fatalism stemming from the 9/11 attacks and the government's successful efforts to inject into the American psyche the threat of random terror. The color-coded terrorist alert system lights up when the administration needs more support for White House policy and legislation. The president regularly warns Americans in high-profile events, "The enemy is wounded but still resourceful and actively recruiting and still dangerous. We cannot afford a moment of complacency." The "servants of evil who plotted the attacks" are everywhere, lurking behind trees and under buildings. Fear is like a drug; its effect is the production of docile bodies. Terrorized by their government, Americans have stood by passively while the Bush regime expands the police state at home, through such mechanisms as the Patriot Acts,[32] and invaded and occupied two countries. The president and his troops have exploited every opportunity to justify their policy goals on the basis of 9/11. Tragically, Americans have done little to resist them. Yet, progressives can hope that in the weeks and months ahead, as more facts emerge revealing the true motives of the Bush administration, that Americans will recognize that Bush's foreign policy makes daily investments in a more dangerous future world.

NOTES

1. US Central Command typically issues press releases with injuries only when there are deaths, so the actual number of injuries is certainly higher.
2. Richard A. Clarke, *Against All Enemies: Inside America's War on Terrorism* (New York: Free Press, 2004).
3. Richard Heinberg, *The Party's Over: Oil, War and the Fate of Industrial Societies* (Gabriola Island, BC, Canada: New Society Publishers, 2003).
4. The desired routes are through Turkey to the Mediterranean and through Afghanistan to Pakistan, thus bypassing routes through Russia, Azerbaijan, and Iran.
5. To pursue these ends, the industry acquired several high-profile political figures. Zbigniew Brzezinski, former NSA under President Carter, was a consultant for Amoco. Bush's vice president, Dick Cheney, advised Halliburton. Henry Kissinger, the former secretary of state under Presidents Nixon and Ford, and Robert Oakley, former State Department counter-terrorism official, were consultants for Unocal.
6. These statements are from an August 21, 1998 Unocal statement. In a press release dated September 14, 2001 Unocal emphasized, "The company is not supporting the Taliban in Afghanistan in any way whatsoever. Nor do we have any project or involvement in Afghanistan."
7. Khalilzad headed the Bush–Cheney transition team for the Department of Defense and served as Counselor to Secretary of Defense Donald Rumsfeld. Under George Bush Sr, he served as assistant under secretary of defense for policy planning. Before that, he served under Reagan from 1985 to 1989 at the Department of State, where he advised the White House on the Iran–Iraq war and the Soviet war in Afghanistan.
8. *The Washington Quarterly* (Winter 2000).
9. Lukoil (Russia) negotiated a multi-billion-dollar deal with Iraq in 1997 to develop the West Qurna field in south Iraq. As late as 2001, Total Fina Elf (France) was negotiating to develop the Majnoon field near the border of Iran.
10. Dan Morgan and David B. Ottaway, "In Iraq War Scenario, Oil is Key Issue: US Drillers Eye Huge Petroleum Pool," *The Washington Post*, September 15, 2002, A1.
11. Janine Zacharia, "Arik's American Front," *The Jerusalem Post*, (January 5, 2001), 4B.
12. Janine Zacharia, "Next Stop, Baghdad?" *Jerusalem Post* (October 12, 2001), 1B.
13. PNAC's list of contributors includes the John M. Olin Foundation (munitions and chemicals interests, with Samuel Huntington directing its Institute for Strategic

Studies), the Sarah Scaife Foundation (big oil), and The Lynde and Harry Bradley Foundation (Reagan's Star Wars project).

14. Although Defense organized DPB as an independent advisory body, Rumsfeld appoints its members and they have access to classified information. Members of the board include former House Speaker Newt Gingrich, former Secretary of State Henry Kissinger, and former CIA Director, Jim Woolsey. DPB advises Rumsfeld and Wolfowitz through former Reagan Defense Department official Douglas Feith.

15. *Time* Magazine, January 27, 2003.

16. Caroline Glick, "A Return to Jacksonian Zionism," *The Jerusalem Post* (November 22, 2002), 1A.

17. Due to conflicts of interest, Perle resigned that position. However, he remained a board member until the spring of 2004. He left the board claiming that he did not want to burden the president's re-election campaign with his provocative ideas.

18. Zacharia, "Next Stop, Baghdad?"

19. Peter Slevin and Glenn Frankel, "If US Wants to Engage, Analysts see Many Options," *The Washington Post* (March 31, 2003), A17.

20. Alan Sipress, "Bush Assures Sharon on US Role in Talks," *The Washington Post* (March 21, 2001), A22.

21. *Jerusalem Post* writer Janine Zacharia in a fall 2001 editorial, "Next Stop, Baghdad?"

22. Frances Fitzgerald, "Threat of War: How Hawks Captured the White House," *The Guardian* (September 24, 2002), 4.

23. Philip Dine, "US Role as Mediator is Questioned," *St. Louis Post Dispatch* (April 21, 2002), A10.

24. Mike Allen, "White House and Hill State Support for Israel: Lobby's Meeting Draws Strong Backing," *The Washington Post*, (April 23, 2001), A11.

25. Prominent right-wing Christians outside of government, such as Jerry Falwell, Pat Robertson, Oral Roberts, and Ralph Reed, as well as organizations such as the National Unity Coalition for Israel, have been vocal in opposing Palestinian statehood. In 1997, these groups launched a major public relations campaign, publishing an advertisement in *The New York Times* declaring, "Christians Call for a United Jerusalem." According to the ad, Israel has a divine right to Jerusalem.

26. Julian Borger, "How I Created the Axis of Evil," *The Guardian* (January 28, 2003), p. 6.

27. Deborah Caldwell, "Does the President Believe he has a Divine Mandate?" *The Times Union* (February 16, 2003).

28. Aaron Latham, "How George W. Found God," *George Magazine* (September 2000).

29. Borger, "How I Created the Axis of Evil."

30. As Bush's first term wears on, Rove has increasingly come to believe that Powell is operating beyond the control of the White House and that the secretary of state is going about his business with a sense of entitlement. "It's constantly, you know, 'I'm in charge, and this is all politics, and I'm going to win the internecine political game,'" Rove has mocked Powell privately.

31. This argument is an echo of points made by Joseph Cirincione of the Carnegie International Institute for Strategic Studies during an interview by the National Public Radio, January 28, 2003.

32. An acronym for "United and Strengthening America by Providing Appropriate Tools Required to Intercept and Obstruct Terrorism."

3
September 11 and the Bush Administration: Compelling Evidence for Complicity

Walter E. Davis

INTRODUCTION

The terrorist attacks on the World Trade Center and Pentagon, on September 11, 2001, have served as a pretext for draconian measures of repression at home, including a cabinet-level Department of Homeland Security, the Patriot Act 1, and its sequel. September 11 (9/11) also became the cause for numerous other acts in the US from massive increases in military spending to a Fast Track Trade Agreement for President Bush. More importantly, 9/11 serves as a pretext for a never-ending war against the world, including pre-emptive strikes against defenseless, but resource-rich countries.

Yet numerous aspects regarding the official stories about 9/11 do not fit with known facts, contradict each other, defy common sense, and indicate a pattern of misinformation and cover-up. The official reports coming out of Washington do very little to answer these concerns. For example, the Congressional report released on July 25, 2003 by a joint panel of House and Senate Intelligence Committees concluded that 9/11 resulted from CIA and FBI "lapses." While incompetence is frightening enough given a $40 billion annual budget for intelligence, it is simply not consistent with the known facts. It is consistent with the reports from other government scandals such as the Warren Commission's Report and the report from the Iran/Contra affair, which produced damage control and cover-up but no answers to the more probing questions. But perhaps a comparison to Watergate is more *à propos* since the Bush administration refuses to release 28 pages of the Congressional report. The report from the Federal Emergency Management Agency (FEMA) is believable unless you are seriously interested in the truth.

Under more careful scrutiny, some answers seem impossible, most are based on speculation, and still other important answers are completely omitted.

Even after more than two years, investigations stop far too short, the public is left in the dark on too many questions that could be easily answered, and no one in the Bush administration has been held accountable for any actions surrounding the attacks of 9/11. The National Commission on Terrorists Attacks Upon the United States (NCTA), formed at the insistence of the families of some of the victims, has likewise failed to answer many of the questions asked by these families and many others. I believe the truth will be exposed only if tremendous public pressure is brought to bear from numerous sources to demand accountability from the Bush administration. It is well known that the US corporate media ask few probing questions, which aids in government cover up. But why there has been so little coverage in the alternative press, with obvious exceptions, is a mystery. The failure of accountability should be a national and international scandal. Questions of why journalists and others in the mass media are failing the people of the US and the world need to be answered.

What this chapter shows is that government agencies knew of impending attacks and were capable of preventing them, but did nothing; their accounts of the events contain contradictions and lies; and they are going to great lengths to prevent any investigation. They are reaping tremendous rewards, including those consistent with previously laid-out plans for the US to maintain its imperial hegemony through the military, economic, and political takeover of Eurasia. Although the degree to which this administration is pursuing a course of world domination at any cost is unprecedented, the course is consistent with the long history of US imperialism and atrocities. One of the best ways of halting this destructive course is to expose the Bush administration and insist on its accountability to the victims' families, the American people, and the people of the world.

The evidence presented in this chapter suggests that the most plausible explanation of the events surrounding 9/11, is that the Bush administration was complicit in the terrorist attacks and has orchestrated its cover-up. The sources cited contain extensive detailed information, additional sources, and analyses beyond what it is possible to provide in this summary.

EVIDENCE OF COMPLICITY BY THE
BUSH ADMINISTRATION IN 9/11 ATTACKS

Here is the US official story as reported by the US corporate media. On the morning of September 11, 2001 four Boeing passenger jets were hijacked within an hour by 19 Arab terrorists armed with box cutters. Pilots among these terrorists took control of the commercial planes and changed course towards targets in New York City and Washington DC. Two of the planes were deliberately crashed into the World Trade Center, causing fires within the Twin Towers that melted the steel support structures, thereby causing the buildings to collapse. A third plane was deliberately crashed into the Pentagon. Passengers on the fourth plane overpowered the hijackers and caused the plane to crash in Pennsylvania. This was an attack on America planned and directed by Osama bin Laden as the leader of al Qaeda, a previously obscure anti-US international terrorist organization composed mainly of Arabs.

This story cries out for further explanations, but nothing official is forthcoming. People are simply expected to believe the official version without question.

THE BUSH ADMINISTRATION KNEW
OF THE 9/11 ATTACKS IN ADVANCE

There are several major sources of evidence to conclude beyond reasonable doubt that numerous people, in the US and around the world, were aware of the possibility of a terrorist attack on the US, and contrary to their claims, the Bush administration was not caught by surprise. First, the entire US intelligence community knew of the 9/11 attacks beforehand, including the fact that commercial jets were to be used as bombs; they also knew the approximate dates and possible targets.[1] Western intelligence had been aware of plans for such terrorist attacks on US soil as early as 1995. The plan, called "Project Bojinka," was known to both the CIA and FBI and was described in court documents in the trial in New York of Ramzi Yousef and Abdul Murad for their participation in the 1993 bombing of the World Trade Center (WTC).

As early as 1996, the FBI was following the activities of Arab students at US flight schools. Several people later identified by the FBI as the hijackers, including Khalid Almihdar and Nawaf Alhazmi along with the man alleged to be the principal organizer, Mohammed Atta, were under active surveillance by US agents prior to 9/11. Several weeks

before the attack, all internal US security agencies were warned of
the impending al Qaeda attacks. The Federal Aviation Administration
(FAA) was warned of the possible attack but did nothing to beef up
security. At least two weeks prior to 9/11 FBI agents again confirmed
that an attack on Lower Manhattan was imminent. Some field agents
predicted, almost precisely, what happened on September 11.[2]

There are numerous other reasons to dismiss as a lie the claim that the
9/11 plane hijackings and attacks caught the US government agencies
by surprise—a rather ominous admission in the first place. For example,
an expert panel commissioned by the Pentagon in 1993 discussed how
an airplane could be used as a bomb. Notably, US security officials had
considered and prepared for possible attacks by suicide planes during
the Atlanta Summer Olympics in 1996. Three incidents took place in
1994, including the stolen single-engine Cessna which crashed into a
tree in the White House grounds just short of the president's bedroom,
and an aborted plan to crash a plane into the Eiffel Tower. As early as
1997, Russia, France, Israel, the Philippines, and Egypt had all warned
the US of the possibility of the attacks. Warning came from several
others sources as well. On May 25, 2002, CBS revealed that President
Bush had been warned in an intelligence briefing on August 6, 2001
that bin Laden might be planning to hijack commercial planes for an
attack in the US.

Second, selected people were told *not* to fly that day. *Newsweek*
(September 24, 2001) reported that on September 10, "a group of
top Pentagon officials suddenly canceled travel plans for the next
morning, apparently because of security concerns" (p. 26). Yet this
same information was not made available to the 266 people who died
onboard the four hijacked commercial aircraft. A significant number
of other people were warned about flying or reporting for work at the
WTC. These include San Francisco Mayor Willie Brown, who received a
phone call eight hours before the hijacking warning him not to travel by
air. Salman Rushdie, under 24-hour protection from Scotland Yard, was
also prevented from flying that day. Ariel Sharon canceled his address
to Israeli support groups in New York City the day before his scheduled
September 11 address. John Ashcroft stopped flying on public airplanes
in July 2001. These revelations are indisputable evidence that people
knew about the impending attacks.

Third, revelations of profits made by insider trading relating to the
9/11 attacks point to the top levels of US business and the CIA.[3] The
intelligence community regularly analyses financial transactions for any
suspicious activity. Only three trading days before September 11, an
inordinate number of "put" options (bets that a stock will go down) were

placed on the stocks of American and United Airlines, the companies whose planes were hijacked in the attacks of 9/11. No such speculation was made on any other airline. Moreover, similar speculation occurred on other companies housed in the World Trade Center, including Merrill Lynch and Morgan Stanley Dean Witter & Co. It is noteworthy that some of the put options were purchased through Deutsche Bank/Alex Brown, a firm managed until 1998 by the current executive director of the CIA, A. B. "Buzzy" Krongard. The *New York Times* reported that Mayo Shattuck III resigned as head of the Alex Brown unit of Deutsche Bank on September 15, 2001.

These multiple, massive, and unprecedented financial transactions show unequivocally that the investors behind these trades were speculating in anticipation of a mid-September 2001 catastrophe that would involve both United and American Airlines and offices in the Twin Towers. To date, both the Securities and Exchange Commission and the FBI have been tight-lipped about their investigations of trades. The names of the investors remain undisclosed and $5 million in profit-taking remains unclaimed in the Chicago Exchange account. A probe could isolate the investors. However, this case has recently been closed without any report being made public or anyone being held accountable. The insider-trading incident further establishes the fact that important people knew in advance of the possible attacks, did nothing about them, and are now covering them up.

EMERGENCY PROCEDURES WERE NOT FOLLOWED

There is incontrovertible evidence that the US air force across the country was comprehensively "stood down" on the morning of 9/11. Routine security measures, normally in place, which may well have prevented the attacks or reduced their impact, were suspended while the attacks were in progress and reinstated once they were over.[4] The sequence of events for each hijacked plane is as follows:

> 7:59 a.m.: *American Airlines Flight 11* leaves Boston's Logan Airport bound for Los Angeles;
> 8:20 a.m.: it is hijacked and goes off course;
> 8:46 a.m.: it smashes into the North Tower of the WTC;
> 10:28 a.m.: the tower completely collapses.

> 8:01 a.m.: *United Airlines Flight 93* sits on the ground for 41 minutes before leaving from Newark bound for San Francisco;

9:20 a.m.: the FAA notifies NORAD that Flight 93 has been hijacked;

9:35 a.m.: the plane goes off course near Cleveland, Ohio, where it makes a 135-degree turn, and heads to the southeast;

10:10 a.m.: it crashes in Shanksville, Pennsylvania.

8:14 a.m.: *United Airlines Flight 175* leaves from Boston bound for Los Angeles;

8:49 a.m.: it deviates from its flight path;

9:03 a.m.: it smashes into the South Tower;

9:59 am. The tower completely collapses.

8:20 a.m.: *American Airlines Flight 77* leaves from Dulles International, 30 miles west of Washington, DC bound for Los Angeles;

8:56 a.m.: transponder signal stops. It goes off course and starts making a 180-degree turn over southern Ohio/northeastern Kentucky;

9:38 a.m.: it allegedly hits the Pentagon.

Andrews Air Force Base is a huge military installation about twelve miles from the Pentagon. On 9/11 two entire squadrons of combat-ready fighter jets at Andrews failed to do their job of protecting the skies over Washington, DC. Despite over one hour's advance warning of a terrorist attack in progress, not a single Andrews' fighter tried to protect the city. The FAA, NORAD, and the military have cooperative procedures enabling fighter jets to intercept commercial aircraft under emergency conditions. They do not need instructions from the White House to intercept commercial aircraft, yet these procedures were not followed.

Within 35 minutes of American Airline Flight 11 departing from Boston's Logan Airport it stopped responding to ground control, and radar indicated that the plane had deviated from its flight path. Two airline attendants on Flight 11 had separately called American Airlines reporting a hijacking, the presence of weapons, and the infliction of injuries on passengers and crew. Yet, according to NORAD's official timeline, NORAD was not contacted until 20 minutes later at 8:40 a.m. Tragically, the fighter jets may not have been deployed until a full 32 minutes after the loss of contact with Flight 11.

Flights 175, 77, and 93 all had this same pattern of delays in notification and in scrambling fighter jets—delays that are difficult to imagine considering that one plane had, by this time, already hit the WTC. The official account of the plane striking the Pentagon is particularly incomprehensible. After it was known that Flight 77 had a problem, it was nevertheless able to change course and fly towards Washington, for about 45 minutes, fly past the White House, and crash into the Pentagon, without any attempt at interception. All the while two squadrons of fighter aircraft were stationed just twelve miles from the eventual target. Since the plane left Dulles Airport, which is close to the Pentagon, why would hijackers fly for 40 minutes away from the intended target and then 40 minutes back unless they believed there was no chance of being intercepted?

Moreover, well-established emergency protocols were not followed by the chairman of the Joint Chiefs of Staff, the secretary of defense, or the president. Acting chairman of the Joint Chiefs of Staff, General Richard B. Myers, stated that he saw a TV report about a plane hitting the WTC but thought it was a small plane, so he went ahead with his meeting with Senator Max Cleland. By the time he came out of the meeting the Pentagon had been hit. Why did General Myers not know about the emergency until it was too late? Secretary of Defense Donald Rumsfeld was at his desk when AA77 crashed into the Pentagon. How is it possible that the National Military Command Center (NMCC), located in the Pentagon and in contact with law enforcement and air traffic controllers from 8:46 a.m., did not communicate to the secretary of defense, also at the Pentagon, about the other hijacked planes, especially the one headed to Washington?[5] After Secretary Rumsfeld was notified, why did he go to the War Room?

The actions of President Bush, while the attacks were occurring, were particularly suspicious because he did not do anything reasonably expected of a president required to protect US citizens and property. The Secret Service is required to inform the president immediately of any national emergency. Yet the president was permitted by the Secret Service to remain in the Sarasota elementary school. At 9:05 a.m., 19 minutes after the first attack and two minutes after the second attack on the WTC, Andrew Card, the presidential chief of staff, whispered something in Bush's ear. At that time the president did not react as if he was interested in trying to do something about the situation. He did not leave the school, convene an emergency meeting, consult with anybody, or intervene in any way to ensure that the air force completed its job. The president's approval is not required for an intercept, but it is required for commercial planes to be shot down.

Yet, Bush did not even attend to the extraordinary events occurring in New York, but simply continued with the reading class. It was not until 20 minutes after the second tower had been hit that he met privately with National Security advisor Condoleezza Rice, FBI director Robert

S. Mueller III, and New York governor George Pataki. At 9:30 a.m., he made an announcement to the press using the same words his father had used ten years earlier: "Terrorism against our nation will not stand." His own explanations of his actions that day contradict known facts.

In the case of a national emergency, seconds of indecision could cost thousands of lives; and it is precisely for this reason that the government has a whole network of adjuncts and advisors to ensure that these top officials are among the first to be informed, not the last. Where were these individuals who did not properly inform the top officials? In short, the CIA, the DCI, the State Department, the president and key figures around him in the White House were ultimately responsible for doing *nothing* in the face of the mounting evidence of an impending threat to US national security. Nafeez Ahmed states that these acts are "indicative of a scale of negligence amounting to effective complicity" (2002, p. 167). Incompetence is a highly improbable explanation.

THE ALLEGED TERRORISTS IN US FLIGHT SCHOOLS?

There are numerous questions regarding the alleged terrorists, including who they were, how they were able to board the planes, and whether in fact they were even on the planes.[6] The names of the alleged terrorists were not on the passenger lists released by the airlines. Photos of the alleged hijackers appeared on the FBI website not long after 9/11, but have since been removed. Both the British and US media reported that several of the individuals, identified as hijackers by the FBI, have been found alive. Thierry Meyssan noted that "Prince Saud Al-Faisal, the Saudi Foreign Minister, declared to the press that, '*It has been proven that five of the persons named in the FBI's list had no connection with what happened*'" (2002, pp. 54–5, emphasis in the original). Indeed, how was it possible for the FBI to be taken by surprise and then produce the names of the alleged hijackers within 24 hours following the attacks? Two possibilities are that the FBI made up the names or assisted the hijackers in boarding the planes. There are reports of several rather bizarre coincidences of the alleged hijackers leaving blatantly conspicuous clues. For example, one outrageous claim is that Mohamed Atta's passport was found at Ground Zero.

If the 19 alleged terrorists did board the planes, the US security agencies should have stopped them from entering this country for intelligence reasons, prior to 9/11, according to the testimony of Mindy Kleinberg during the hearings of NCTA. Fifteen of the 19 hijackers' visas should have been unquestionably denied because their applications were incomplete and incorrect. Most of the alleged hijackers were young, unmarried, and unemployed. They were, in short, the "classic over-stay candidates." A seasoned former consular officer stated in the *National Review* magazine, "Single, idle young adults with no specific destination in the United States rarely get visas absent compelling circumstances."[7]

There are several cases damaging to the credibility of the official accounts of 9/11. But the US response to Mohammed Atta, the alleged lead hijacker, is most extraordinary.[8] The FBI had been monitoring Atta's movements for several months in 2000. According to PBS's *Frontline*, the Immigration and Naturalization Service failed on three occasions to stop Atta from entering the US on a tourist visa in 2001, even though officials knew the visa had expired in 2000, and that Atta had violated its terms by taking flight lessons. Furthermore, Atta had already been implicated in a terrorist bombing in Israel, with the information passed on to the United States before he was first issued his tourist visa.

Another important aspect, as Daniel Hopsicker and Thierry Messyan have documented, is that many of the alleged terrorist pilots received their initial training in Venice, Florida at one of the flight schools of highly questionable credibility and with approval of US intelligence. Mohammed Atta attended International Officers School at Maxwell Air Force Base in Montgomery, Alabama; Abdulaziz Alomari had attended Aerospace Medical School at Brooks Air Force Base in Texas; Saeed Alghamdi had been to the Defense Language Institute in Monterey, California. These are all names of identified hijackers, but the US government has denied the match. Three days after the 9/11 attacks, FBI director Robert S. Mueller III claimed that these findings were new and had not been known by the FBI previously. This is a lie.

Zacarias Moussaoui was arrested after his flight trainers at the Minnesota flight school, Pan Am International Flight Academy, reported highly suspicious behavior. He was greatly unqualified; he wanted to learn to fly a 747 but was not interested in takeoffs or landings; he was traveling on a French passport and, when contacted, the French said he was a suspected terrorist connected to al Qaeda. A special counter-terrorism panel of the FBI and CIA reviewed the case but did not pursue it. Subsequently, Moussaoui was arrested as the "twentieth" hijacker, but was again released without charge. Government prosecutors dropped charges rather than allow Moussaoui to interview the three top al Qaeda suspects captured by the United States. Corporate media have largely ignored this story.

There are numerous glaring anomalies, illegalities, and scandals connected with Wally Hilliard and Rudi Dekkers' Huffman Aviation

School at Venice, Florida, where other hijackers trained. Dekkers had no aviation experience and was under indictment in his native country, The Netherlands, on financial charges. He purchased his aviation school at just about the time the alleged terrorists moved into town and began their lessons. He has yet to be investigated, even though he initially trained some of the accused hijackers.

According to Hopsicker, Britannia Aviation was awarded a five-year contract to run a large regional maintenance facility at Lynchburg at a time when the company had few assets, employees, or corporate history and did not possess the necessary FAA license to perform the maintenance. Britannia was a company with known CIA connections. It was operating illegally out of Huffman Aviation, the flight school that trained al Qaeda hijackers and was given a "green light" from the Justice Department's Drug Enforcement Administration, and the local Venice Police Department was warned to "leave them alone."

One answer to the question of how the accused terrorists entered the US with ease is that the Bush administration made it possible for Saudi visitors to come to the US under a program called US Visa Express, introduced four months before September 11. This was at a time when the US intelligence community was on alert for an imminent al Qaeda attack. Michael Springmann, former head of the Visa Bureau at the US Consulate in Jeddah, Saudi Arabia, said that he was repeatedly ordered by high-level State Department officials to issue visas to unqualified applicants. His complaints to higher authorities at several agencies went unanswered. In a CBC interview, he indicated that the CIA was indeed complicit in the attacks.[9]

Most of the accused hijackers were Saudis, as is Osama bin Laden, and the Saudi Arabian government is known to give financial support to terrorist organizations. Why, then, is Iraq and not Saudi Arabia a target if the US government is concerned about terrorism? The obvious answer seems to be that the Saudi Arabian monarchy has a long-standing cooperative business relationship with US oil and arms industries, possibly including a provision to curtail surveillance on their activities.[10] Iraq at the time of 9/11 had no such cooperative arrangement. There is evidence that Osama bin Laden continues to receive extensive support, not only from members of his own family, but also from members of the Saudi establishment. A *New Statesman* report stated that "bin Laden and his gang are just the tentacles; the head lies safely in Saudi Arabia, protected by US forces." The hijackers the FBI identified as being responsible for 9/11 were not illiterate, bearded fanatics from Afghanistan. They were all educated, highly skilled, middle-class professionals and not the typical kamikaze pilots they are alleged to have been. Of the alleged men involved, 13 were Saudi nationals.

OSAMA BIN LADEN:
MASTERMIND, ACCOMPLICE, OR SET-UP?

Osama bin Laden was unofficially convicted of the attacks within a time-frame too brief to possibly have allowed any genuine supporting intelligence to have been gathered. That is, conviction would not be impossible if they did not already possess that information. Either the charges are contrived or the government agencies had some forewarning of the attacks, even if it was not specific.

It is nearly impossible that bin Laden was involved except in the capacity of complicity with US authorities or at best, in the context of the current administration knowing all along his plans and deliberately allowing him to carry them out. From the beginning no convincing evidence against bin Laden has been made public. Until mid-December, there was nothing but the continued repetition of his name. Steve Grey reports that an official document from the British government detailing allegations against bin Laden provides no convincing evidence. Of the 69 points of "evidence" cited, ten relate to background information about the relationship between bin Laden and the Taliban; 15 relate to background information regarding the general philosophies of al Qaeda, and its relationship to bin Laden; none gives any facts concerning the events of 9/11; and most do not even attempt to directly relate anything mentioned to the events of that day. Twenty-six list allegations relating to previous terrorist attacks. Even if bin Laden were convicted of previous terrorist attacks, it is well known that this fact alone would not stand up in a court of law as evidence for involvement of September 11.

Within less than four hours of the attacks, the media were fed comments that assumed bin Laden's guilt and were made on the basis of events that could not have possibly occurred. The Pentagon and the Department of Defense used dialogue attributed to bin Laden in an effort to incriminate him, while refusing to release all of the dialogue or issue a verbatim, literal translation. On December 13, 2001 the Bush administration offered an alleged "confession" tape as the only evidence, and this has simply been accepted by many in the media and in the general population as sufficient to declare his guilt. But a fake tape is easily produced with today's technology. Thus, against the backdrop of the many reported denials by bin Laden that he was involved in the attacks, there are few reasons to accept this "evidence" as convincing.

Rather, one must ask why was it considered necessary to lie in order to create a case against bin Laden?

⌊What is certain is that Osama bin Laden's picture became the focus of most people in the US, establishing an image of an evil enemy, and thereby creating the important psychological mind-set to accept revenge. This constant barrage of news coverage of bin Laden and al Qaeda also diverted attention from questions about why the attacks were not prevented. Added to this is the fact that today, with the wars in Afghanistan and Iraq declared over, bin Laden, "public enemy number one," is all but forgotten by the US corporate media.

If bin Laden was really the mastermind of the attacks, it is not likely that the FBI agents would have been ordered to curtail their investigation of these attacks on October 10, 2001.[11] Moreover, the FBI was called off its investigation of bin Laden and the Saudi royal family prior to 9/11. Soon after entering the White House, the Bush administration strengthened an existing order to the FBI to "back off" their investigations of Saudi-based terrorist organizations, including the World Assembly of Muslim Youth, headquartered in Falls Church, Virginia, and run by a brother of Osama bin Laden. John O'Neill, the FBI agent who for years led US investigations into bin Laden's al Qaeda network, complained bitterly that the State Department blocked attempts to prove bin Laden's guilt in the bombing of the USS *Cole*. He resigned in protest and became head of security for the World Trade Center, where he was killed on September 11. One law enforcement official was quoted as saying, "The investigative staff has to be made to understand that we're not trying to solve a crime now." The FBI agents were commanded to cut short their investigations into the attacks and those involved. FBI agents were threatened with prosecution under the National Security Act if they publicized information from their investigations. David P. Schippers, noted Chicago lawyer and the House Judiciary Committee's chief investigator in the Clinton impeachment trial, is now representing some of the FBI agents in a suit against the US government in an attempt to enable them to legally tell what they know.

THE OFFICIAL STORY OF 9/11 IS SIMPLY IMPLAUSIBLE

As former German minister of technology, Andreas von Buelow, remarked, "Planning the attacks was a master deed, in technical and organizational terms. To hijack four big airliners within a few minutes and fly them into targets within a single hour and doing so on complicated flight routes! That is unthinkable, without backing from the secret apparatuses of state and industry." Thus, it should not be surprising that many important unanswered questions surround the attacks on the WTC and the Pentagon.

According to some scientists it is not possible for the World Trade Center's Twin Towers to have collapsed in the manner they did as a result of being struck by two jet planes. The first official version, that the burning jet fuel caused the steel girders supporting the Twin Towers to melt, had to be changed when no credible scientific evidence supported it. But subsequent versions are also speculation. The WTC towers were designed to take the impact of a Boeing 707. It is not possible that fire from the jet fuel could have melted the steel girders. South Tower was hit second but fell first. Both towers collapsed evenly and smoothly in a manner consistent with that caused by a planned demolition. Steel buildings are not known to collapse because of fire, and concrete does not turn to powder when it crashes to the ground. Rather, based upon scientific evidences, photos and videos of the event, and reports of scientists, the WTC architect and engineers, it is more convincing that the towers collapsed because of demolition rather than burning jet fuel.[12]

The collapse of the tower known as WTC-7 raises even more questions because it was not hit by anything but debris and yet it collapsed in a manner similar to the Twin Towers only seven hours later.[13] There is record only of small fires seen on a few floors prior to its collapse. No one, including FEMA, has explained why WTC-7 collapsed.

Even more outrageous are the official story and secrecy regarding the Pentagon. The Pentagon is the largest office building in the world (6.5 million square feet of floor space) housing more than 20,000 people. At the time of the attacks, its occupation was normal except for the one section being renovated. The story people are expected to believe is that a large commercial plane was piloted by a hijacker inexperienced in flying, but who nevertheless circled the Pentagon making a 280-degree turn, traveling at approximately 345 mph (555 km/hr), and flew very low to the ground (the Pentagon is 80 feet high) in order to crash orthogonally into the one section being renovated. An aerial view shows that the only sensible way to crash into the Pentagon as a kamikaze is to fly straight on aiming at the center. Also damaging to the official story is the fact that on September 14 the Department of Defense announced that emergency workers had found the two black boxes, but except for small pieces, no plane, luggage, or passenger debris was recovered. The military first denied that there were any videos of the crash and then produced five images after French investigator Thierry Meyssan's (2002) book showed the improbability of the official account.

Mystery also surrounds the plane crash in Shanksville, Pennsylvania. The most obvious question concerns the remains of the plane and its passengers, which seem to have vanished in thin air. Who were the passengers aboard Flight 93? The official reports of cell phone contact with passengers of Flight 93 are highly unlikely given recent research and expert testimony.[14] No recording of these calls has been made public. Also, what was the explosion reported by some of the local people who witnessed the crash? Another eyewitness reported seeing a white plane resembling a fighter jet circling the site just after the crash. As in the case of Ground Zero, no one has been allowed near the site.

It is well known that bin Laden's close working relationship with the CIA began in the 1980s. The claim is that they have since fallen out, but this story is a lie. Indeed, on October 31, the French daily *Le Figaro* reported that while in a Dubai hospital receiving treatment for a chronic kidney infection in July 2001, Osama bin Laden met with a top CIA official. The bin Laden and Bush families have maintained close business ties through the Carlyle Group. Some of the members of the bin Laden family and the Saudi royal family were in the US during the attack and were flown out shortly after. George Bush Sr met with Shafiq bin Laden, one of Osama's brothers, on September 10 in Washington, DC at a Carlyle Group business conference. According to the corporate media spin, this is OK, because the rest of the family has disowned Osama for his terrorist activities and anti-US views. The evidence amply confirms that the CIA never severed its ties to the Islamic Militant Network. Since the end of the Cold War these covert intelligence links have not only been maintained, they have become increasingly sophisticated.

If bin Laden was an enemy of the US, he could have been captured before 9/11 and should have been captured since. There have been several opportunities to capture him after declaring him wanted for the 1993 bombing of the WTC, but no effort to do so was made.[15] Prior to 9/11, the FBI attributed the attacks on the embassies in Nairobi and Dar-es-Salaam to Osama bin Laden and offered a $5 million ransom. Sudan offered to assist the Clinton administration in capturing bin Laden, but was ignored. It was also reported that bin Laden was meeting with the CIA as late as July 2001 (while in the American Hospital in Dubai). An examination of US efforts to capture Osama bin Laden shows they have in fact, with the help of two allies, Saudi Arabia and the United Arab Emirates, consistently blocked attempts to investigate and capture him. Eleven bin Laden family members were flown safely out of the same Boston airport where the hijacking took place a few days earlier.

Why were family members of the most wanted man in America not detained for questioning?

AN ALTERNATIVE STORY TIES THE ALLEGED TERRORISTS TO THE CIA AND PAKISTAN'S ISI

It is most likely that Pakistan's Inter Services Intelligence (ISI) was directly involved in 9/11.[16] The links between al Qaeda, Pakistan's ISI and the CIA, and between the ISI, Osama bin Laden and the Taliban axis are a matter of public record. The CIA also has close cooperative links with Mossad (Israeli intelligence) which also may have played an important role in 9/11. Pakistan has long been a supporter of al Qaeda. The ISI has been a mechanism by which the CIA indirectly channeled support to al Qaeda and has been used by successive US administrations as a "go-between." Pakistan's military intelligence apparatus constitutes the core institutional support to both Osama bin Laden's al Qaeda and the Taliban. Without this institutional support, there would have been no Taliban government in Kabul. In turn, without the support of the US government, there would be no powerful military intelligence apparatus in Pakistan.

It was reported that ISI's director-general, General Mahmoud Ahmad, had funneled $100,000 to the alleged lead hijacker, Mohammed Atta, shortly before September 11. The US government protected him, and itself, by asking him to resign after the discovery, thus blocking a further inquiry and a potential scandal. In the wake of 9/11, the Bush administration consciously sought the "cooperation" of the ISI, which had been supporting and abetting Osama bin Laden and the Taliban. In other words, the Bush administration's relations with Pakistan's ISI, including its "consultations" with General Mahmoud Ahmad in the week prior to September 11, raise the issues of cover-up and complicity. While Ahmad was talking to US officials at the CIA and the Pentagon, the ISI allegedly had contacts with the 9/11 terrorists.

THOSE WHO BENEFITED THE MOST FROM 9/11

The 9/11 attacks came at an extremely fortuitous time for the Bush administration, the Pentagon, the CIA, the FBI, the weapons industry, and the oil industry, all of which have benefited immensely from this tragedy, as has Israel. It is worth noting the astute observations of Canadian social philosopher John McMurtry: "To begin with, the forensic principle of 'who most benefits from the crime?' clearly points in the direction of the Bush administration. ... The more you

connections and the sweeping lapse of security across so
dinates, the more the lines point backwards"]to the White
you add "follow the money," one trail goes from the CIA to
Pakistan's ISI to al Qaeda, and another trail goes from US taxpayers
to particular players in the military-industrial complex connected to
the Bush administration.

The 9/11 disaster has resulted in power and profit at home and abroad
by both the bin Laden and the Bush families. There are significant
business ties between bin Laden and senior members of the Bush
administration through the Carlyle Group, the giant private and
secretive investment firm managing some $14 billion in assets, including
many defense-related companies. Carlyle employs George Bush Sr, and
has long-standing financial ties to the bin Laden family. So while there
is compelling evidence that Osama bin Laden has not broken from his
family, it is also a matter of record that the Bush administration is in turn
very significantly tied to the same family. Reports have emerged that the
Carlyle Group, Halliburton, and many other firms with ties to the Bush
administration have profited immensely from the wars in Afghanistan
and Iraq and from the militarization of US foreign policy.

Israel is the regional watchdog for the West but is also dependent on
the US for its security. Clearly it benefits from the US occupation of
one of its most feared enemies. It may also now share in some of the
benefits from the world's second largest oil reserve.

Two further arguments support the contention that the Bush
administration's complicity in 9/11, but the details are given in other
chapters of this volume. First, it is recognized that the wars on Afghanistan
and Iraq were planned prior to 9/11 as revealed in documents from the
Project for a New American Century and in Zbigniew Brzezinski's "The
Grand Chessboad." Second, there are well-documented precedents for
government acts of complicity and fabrications.[17]

LIES, SECRECY, AND COVER-UP

There has never been a single event in the history of the US republic
which has received more media coverage. Moreover, there were 2,952
people killed in the 2001 World Trade Center attacks, more civilian deaths
on a single day than at any other time. In spite of the unprecedented
magnitude of death and destruction in New York on 9/11, the US
government spent only $600,000 for its single study of the causes for
the Twin Towers collapses. Compare this to the $40 million that was
spent investigating Bill Clinton's activities with Monica Lewinksy in
1988–99 and the only rational conclusion is that there is no desire on

the part of the Bush administration for the public to know the truth about 9/11.

The lies of the Bush administration are numerous and currently many of them are well publicized, including Bush's claim that he saw on TV one of the planes crashing into the tower before any video was ever shown. This was just one of Bush's seven different "recalls" of the events on September 11. The statements of the FAA, NORAD, the air force pilots, and traffic controllers conflict, contradict known facts, and defy reason. In spite of this deliberate deception, the mass media have made very little of the fact that from the beginning, the Bush administration has vigorously attempted to thwart any investigation into the circumstances of the attack.

Airline crashes are routinely investigated with great thoroughness, and the results released to the public. By contrast, the Bush administration has barred virtually any release of information about 9/11. For nearly six months, it blocked Congressional hearings and rejected calls for a special commission of inquiry. The White House finally worked out a deal with the Democratic and Republican Congressional leaders to consign the investigation to hearings held jointly by the House and Senate intelligence committees but continued its intimidations.

The joint Congressional hearings were held behind closed doors, and their 800-page secret report detailing the intelligence and law enforcement failures that preceded the attacks (including provocative, if unheeded warnings, given to President Bush and his top advisors during the summer of 2001) was completed in December 2003. Yet only a bare-bones list of "findings" with virtually no details has been made public. But nearly six months later, a "working group" of Bush administration intelligence officials assigned to review the document has taken a hard line against further public disclosure. By refusing to declassify many of its most significant conclusions, the administration has essentially thwarted Congressional plans to release the report. The intelligence officials' attempt to reclassify other aspects of the report seems ludicrous. As noted at the beginning of this chapter, only because the families of some of the victims of 9/11 were persistent was an independent commission formed. After stonewalling, the White House, incredibly, appointed Henry Kissinger as its head. He resigned shortly after. With New Jersey governor Thomas Kean finally appointed to lead the commission, questions of conflict of interest remain. Even so, the White House wrestled with the Kean Commission, refusing to release necessary documents.

It is also noteworthy that officials in the Bush administration illegally removed pages from the Iraq UN report, pages that are believed to identify those who supplied Saddam Hussein's regime with weapons of mass destruction and training on how to use them. These acts are not isolated, unfortunate mistakes, but demonstrate a consistent pattern. While President George W. Bush and Attorney General John Ashcroft call for more and more intrusive surveillance capabilities on citizens of the US, they themselves operate in unprecedented secrecy.

The Federal Emergency Management Agency's failure to investigate and its cover-up are truly beyond belief. Only a team of volunteer investigators was assembled, then given no funding and not allowed to go to Ground Zero. People were threatened with arrest if they took pictures at the two sites of the attack and the site of the plane crash in Pennsylvania. Instead of being made available to the investigating team, the debris from the collapsed Twin Towers was removed from the site without forensic examination and sold to scrap merchants overseas with pledges of secrecy about the contents. Controlled Demolition Inc. of Phoenix, Maryland was one of the site's main clean-up management contractors and their plan for recycling the steel was accepted.

The Securities and Exchange Commission refused to report on its insider trading investigation into people who made millions from the 9/11 tragedy. As part of the cover-up there have been constant distractions away from the real issues of 9/11 with such media headlines as orange alerts, anthrax attacks, and CIA agent exposures. Moreover, the reasonable calls for an investigation into the events surrounding 9/11, made by US Congressional Representatives Nancy Pelosi and Cynthia McKinney inspired the kind of outrage that is generally motivated by a desire to suppress rather than reveal the truth.

SUMMARY AND CONCLUSION

If government agencies knew of the impending attacks, were capable of preventing them, but did nothing, their accounts of the events contained contractions and lies; they went to great lengths to prevent any investigation and subsequently reaped tremendous benefits, what should be concluded? The evidence seems clear that if the many agencies of the US government had done their jobs, the 9/11 attacks most likely would have been prevented. If there had been an immediate investigation into 9/11, the wars on Afghanistan and Iraq could not have been justified simply on the basis of terrorism. Surely questions must be asked as to why no one in any of the government agencies has been held accountable, and why journalists and others in the mass media are not held responsible for the cover-up, deception, and lack of investigative reporting. Given the evidence presented it is not surprising that public whistleblowing is beginning to emerge. It remains to be seen what will happen with the pending class action lawsuits being brought against persons in the administration for letting 9/11 happen.

One important insight into conspiracy theories concerns how hierarchical authoritarian social systems function. Top-down directives and commands, especially if they carry the weight of threats of censorship and punishment, serve to keep any dissent in check. There is a great deal of self-censorship operating in all institutions in the US. Shared ideology, or perhaps more specifically what social psychologists in studies of organizational behavior call "groupthink," also plays a major role among the decision-makers. Groupthink is decision-making characterized by uncritical acceptance of and conformity to the prevailing view. Thus, the will of a few key people can be spread within and across government agencies.

Thus the possibility of complicity on the part of the Bush administration is very real. Past history, as well as the currently established facts, is on the side of those raising this possibility. At the very least, further and more honest investigations must take place and some accountability exacted from those responsible. _ Solution

It seems apropos to conclude (I paraphrase): "if you are part of the problem, then you are not part of the solution." Thus the solution lies with the people themselves and not with any US government agency, least of all the Executive. It is critical to appeal to the several important alternative media outlets who have bought into the official story of "blowback," to reconsider their position. It took 25 years for Robert B. Stinnett[18] to bring to conclusion the evidence showing Roosevelt's involvement in Pearl Harbor. Will it take 25 years before the truth of 9/11 is brought to light? Are the efforts of Stinnett and others to be for naught?

ACKNOWLEDGEMENT

I would like to thank Ed Rippy, Paul Wolf, Karen Capel, Marta Steele, J. Walter Plinge, and Timothy Chandler for their helpful comments.

NOTES

1.   There are numerous sources for this. Consult Nafeez Mosaddeq Ahmed, *The War on Freedom: How and Why America was attacked September 11, 2001* (Joshua Tree, CA: Tree of Life Publications, 2002), chapter 4; John W. Dean, "The 9/11 Report Raises More Serious Questions About The White House Statements On Intelligence", http://writ.news.findlaw.com/dean/20030729.html, 2003; Alex Jones at www. infowars.com and www.rense.com; Thierry Meyssan, *9/11 The Big Lie* (London:

Carnot Publishing, 2002); Ed Rippy, http://erippy.home.mindspring.com; and "9–11 and U.S. global hegemony," http://www.globalresearch.ca/articles/RIP207A.html; Michael Ruppert, From the Wilderness Publications, 2002. http://www.copvcia.com; Paul Joseph Watson, *Order out of Chaos: Elite Sponsored Terrorism & the New World Order* (Austin, TX: Alex Jones Productions, 2003); Marta Steele, "9/11: The Will toward Survival," http://www.legitgov.org/essay_steele_conspiracy_%20theory_911. htm#_ftn6, 2003.

2. Ahmed, *The War on Freedom*, provides a careful documentation of this evidence as reported in numerous media outlets. See also, *Judicial Watch* (September 11, 2002), http://www.judicialwatch.org/2469.shtml. The US government not only tracks suspected terrorists, but also trains and finances them.

3. Ruppert, From the Wilderness Publications; and Daniel Hopsicker, *Barry and the Boys: The CIA, the Mob and America's Secret History* (Eugene, OR: Mad Cow Press, 2001); Rippy, http://erippy.home.mindspring.com, documents the close connection of the CIA to Wall Street, the major international financial institutions, including the infamous BCCI, the arms and drug trade, and organized crime.

4. Ahmed, *The War on Freedom*, Mark R. Elsis, "Stand Down: Exposing NORAD's Wag the 911 Window Dressing Tale": http://StandDown.net (2002); Jared Israel, http://emperors-clothes.com (2001). See also several articles by Jared Israel, John Flaherty, Illarion Bykov, Francisco Gil-White, and George Szamuely; Steve Grey "September 11 Attacks: Evidence of U.S. Collusion," http://austin.indymedia.org/ front.php3?article_id=2342&group=webcast (2002). Paul Thompson, "The failure to Defend the Skies on 9/11": http://www.cooperativeresearch.net/timeline/main/ essayairdefense.html (2003).

5. Note: Instructions issued by the Chairman of the Joint Chiefs of Staff on June 1, 2001. "In the event of a hijacking, the NMCC will be notified by the most expeditious means by the FAA. The NMCC will ... forward requests for DOD assistance to the Secretary of Defense for approval."

6. Mark R. Elsis "36 or 37 Missing, and 70 per cent Empty," http://911Timeline. net/36Or37MissingAnd70PercentEmpty.htm (2003); Meyssan, *9/11 The Big Lie.*

7. Cited by Mindy Kleinberg: http://www.9–11commission.gov/hearings/; www. unansweredquestions.org. See especially the testimony of Mindy Kleinberg, Stephen Push, and others on the First Public Hearings Archives, p. 163.

8. Daniel Hopsicker "9/11: The American connection," http://www.madcowprod.com (2002).

9. "A Canadian Broadcasting Corporation (CBC) interview with Michael Springman exposes CIA Links to Osama BinLaden (January 19, 2001)," http://www. globalresearch.ca/articles/CBC201A.html.

10. This relationship goes back at least 60 years. See especially, Ahmed, *The War on Freedom*; Michel Chossudovsky, *War and Globalisation: The Truth behind September 11* (London: Zed Books, 2002); Rippy, http://erippy.home.mindspring.com.

11. This information is reported in numerous international and some domestic news outlets; see also Jones, www.infowars.com; Patrick Martin "One Year after the Terror Attacks: Still no Official Investigation into 9/11," http://globalresearch.ca/articles/ MAR209A.html (2002); Rippy, http://erippy.home.mindspring.com.

12. Jim Hoffman "Thermodynamic analysis of the Twin Tower collapses," http:// 911research.wtc7.net/papers/dustvolume/volume.html (2003).

13. See especially Jim Hoffman et al.; http://911research.wtc7.net/papers/; Martin Doutré, http://www.nzaif.com/pentagon/pentagon911.html (2001); Gerard Holmgren, "Physical and Mathematical Analysis of the Pentagon Crash," http://

www.serendipity.li/wot/holmgren/index.html (2002); Eric Hufsmidt, *Painful Questions: An Analysis of the September 11th Attack* (Goleta, CA: Eric Hufschmid, 2002); Scott Loughrey "WTC-7: The Improbable Collapse," http://globalresearch. ca/articles/LOU308A.html (2003); Thierry Meyssan, *Pentagate* (London: Carnot, 2002).

14. A.K. Dewdney "Project Achilles' Final Report and Summary of Findings," http:// www.feralnews.com/issues/911/dewdney/project_achilles_report_3_030426.html (2003).

15. Ahmed, *The War on Freedom*; Chossudovsky, *War and Globalization*; Eric Lichtblau "White House Approved Departure of Saudis After Sept. 11, Ex-Aide Says," *New York Times*, September 4, 2003; Meyssan, *9/11 The Big Lie*; Watson, *Order out of Chaos*.

16. Ahmed, *The War on Freedom*; Chaim Kupferberg, "There is something about Omar: Truth, Lies, and the Legend of 9/11," http://globalresearch.ca/articles/KUP310A. html (2003).

17. James Bamford, *Body of Secrets: Anatomy of the Ultra-secret National Security Agency: From the Cold War through the Dawn of a New Century* (New York: Doubleday, 2001). William Peppers, *An Act of State: The Execution of Martin Luther King* (London: Verso, 2003).

18. Robert B. Stinnett, *Day of Deceit: the Truth about FDR and Pearl Harbor* (New York: Touchstone, 2000).

Part II
The Neo-conservative Destruction of American Society

4
Above the Law:
Executive Power after September 11

Alison Parker and Jamie Fellner

GOOD GOVERNMENT UNDER LAW

Since taking office, President George W. Bush has governed as though he had received an overwhelming mandate for policies that emphasize strong executive powers and a distrust—if not outright depreciation—of the role of the judiciary. The Bush administration has frequently taken the position that federal judges too often endorse individual rights at the expense of policies chosen by the Executive or Legislative branches of government, and it has looked to nominate judges who closely share its political philosophy. But the concern is more fundamental than specific judges or decisions. Rather, the administration seems intent on shielding executive actions deemed to promote national security from any serious judicial scrutiny, demanding instead deference from the courts on even the most cherished of rights, the right to liberty.

Much of the US public's concern about post-September 11 policies has focused on the government's new surveillance powers, including the ability to peruse business records, library files, and other data of individuals against whom there may not even be any specific suspicion of complicity with terrorism. These policies potentially affect far more US citizens than, for example, the designation of "enemy combatants," or the decision to hold individuals for months in prison on routine visa charges. But the latter efforts to diminish the right to liberty and to curtail or circumvent the courts' protection of that right may be far more dangerous to the US polity as a whole. Critics of the administration's anti-terrorism efforts have raised concerns that civil liberties are being sacrificed for little benefit in national security. But those critiques have generally failed to grapple with more fundamental questions: who should decide how much protection should be afforded individual rights and who should determine what justice requires—the

Executive or the Judiciary? And who should determine how much the public is entitled to know about domestic anti-terrorist policies that infringe on individual rights?

Many of the Bush administration's post-September 11 domestic strategies directly challenge the role of federal and administrative courts in restraining executive action, particularly action that affects basic human rights. Following September 11, the Bush administration detained over 1,000 people presumed guilty of links to or of having knowledge of terrorist activities, and it impeded meaningful judicial scrutiny of most of those detentions. It has insisted on its right to withhold from the public most of the names of those arrested in connection with its anti-terrorism efforts. It has designated persons arrested in the United States as "enemy combatants" and claims authority to hold them incommunicado in military prisons, without charges or access to counsel. It insists on its sole authority to keep imprisoned indefinitely and virtually incommunicado hundreds of men at its military base at Guantánamo Bay, Cuba, most of whom were taken into custody during the US war in Afghanistan. It has authorized military trials of foreign detainees under rules that eschew a meaningful right of defense and civilian appellate review.

In all of these actions, the Bush administration has put the ancient right to Habeas Corpus under threat, perhaps unsurprisingly since Habeas "has through the ages been jealously maintained by courts of law as a check upon the illegal usurpation of power by the executive."[1] Habeas Corpus, foreshadowed in 1215 in the Magna Carta and enshrined in the US Constitution after centuries of use in England, guarantees every person deprived of his or her liberty a quick and efficacious check by the courts against "all manner of illegal confinement."[2]

The Bush administration argues that national security—the need to wage an all-out "war against terrorism"—justifies its conduct. Of course, there is hardly a government that has not invoked national security as a justification for arbitrary or unlawful arrests and detentions. And there is hardly a government that has not resisted judicial or public scrutiny of such actions. But the administration's actions are particularly troubling and the damage to the rule of law in the United States may be more lasting because it is hard to foresee an endpoint to the terrorist danger that the administration insists warrants its actions. It is unlikely that global terrorism will be defeated in the foreseeable future. Does the US government intend to hold untried detainees for the rest of their lives? Does it intend to keep the public from knowing who has been arrested until the last terrorist is behind bars?

US anti-terrorism policies not only contradict principles woven into the country's political and legal structure, they also contradict international human rights principles. The diverse governmental obligations provided for in human rights treaties can be understood as obligations to treat people justly. The imperative of justice is most explicitly delineated with regard to rights that are particularly vulnerable to the coercive or penal powers of government, such as the right to liberty of person. Human rights law recognizes that individual freedom should not be left to the whim of rulers. To ensure restraints on the arbitrary or wrongful use of a state's power to detain, the International Covenant on Civil and Political Rights (ICCPR), to which the United States is a party, requires that the courts—not the Executive Branch—decide the legality of detention.[3] The ICCPR also establishes specific requirements for court proceedings where a person's liberty is at stake, including that the proceedings be public. Even if there were to be a formally declared state of emergency, restrictions on the right to liberty must be "limited to the extent strictly required by the exigencies of the situation."[4]

Justice cannot exist without respect for human rights. As stated in the preamble of the Universal Declaration of Human Rights, "recognition of the inherent dignity and of the equal and inalienable rights of all members of the human family is the foundation of freedom, justice and peace in the world." The Bush administration's rhetoric acknowledges human rights and insists that the fight against terrorism is a fight to preserve "the non-negotiable demands of human dignity, the rule of law, limits on the power of the state—and equal justice," as President Bush told the graduating class of the West Point military academy in June 2002. But the Bush administration's actions contradict such fine words. Taken together, the Bush administration's anti-terrorism practices represent a stunning assault on basic principles of justice, government accountability, and the role of the courts.

It is as yet unclear whether the courts will permit the Executive Branch to succeed. Faced with the government's incantation of the dangers to national security if it is not allowed to do as it chooses, a number of courts have been all too ready to abdicate their obligation to scrutinize the government's actions and uphold the right to liberty. During previous times of national crisis the US courts have also shamefully failed to protect individual rights—the internment of Japanese Americans during World War II, which received the Supreme Court's seal of approval, being one notorious example. As new cases arising from the government's actions make their way through the judicial process, one must hope that the courts will recognize the unprecedented dangers for human rights and justice posed by the Bush administration's assertion of unilateral power over the lives and liberty of citizens and non-citizens alike.

ARBITRARY DETENTIONS OF VISA VIOLATORS

In a speech shortly after the September 11 attacks, Attorney General John Ashcroft said, "Let the terrorists among us be warned. If you overstay your visa, even by one day, we will arrest you. If you violate a local law, you will be put in jail and kept in custody for as long as possible."[5] The Attorney General carried out his threat, using a variety of strategies to secure the detention of more than 1,200 non-citizens in a few months. We do not know how many, if any, terrorists were included among these detainees. Only a handful was charged with terrorism-related crimes. But we do know that the haphazard and indiscriminate process by which the government swept Arabs and Muslims into custody resulted in hundreds of detentions that could not be effectively reviewed or challenged because the Executive weakened or ignored the usual checks in the immigration system that guard against arbitrary detention.

The right to liberty circumscribes the ability of a government to detain individuals for purposes of law enforcement—including protection of national security. While the right is not absolute, it is violated by arbitrary detentions, i.e., detentions that are either not in accordance with the procedures established by law or which are manifestly disproportional, unjust, unpredictable, or unreasonable. International and US Constitutional law mandates various safeguards to protect individuals from arbitrary detention, including the obligations of authorities to inform detainees promptly of the charges against them; the obligation to permit detainees to be released on bail pending conclusion of legal proceedings in the absence of strong countervailing reasons, such as the individual's danger to the community or flight risk; and the obligation to provide a detainee with effective access to a court to review the legality of the detention. In the case of hundreds of post-September 11 detainees in the United States, the government chose, as a matter of policy and practice, to ignore or weaken these safeguards.

It did so because one of its key post-September 11 strategies domestically was to detain anyone who it guessed might have some connection to past or future terrorist activities, and to keep them incarcerated for as long as necessary to complete its investigations into those possible connections. US criminal law prohibits detention solely for the purpose of investigation, i.e., to determine whether the detained individual knows anything about or is involved in criminal activities.

The law also prohibits "preventive" detentions, incarceration designed to prevent the possibility of future crimes. Detention must be predicated on probable cause to believe the suspect committed, attempted, or conspired to commit a crime. Judges—not the Executive Branch—have the ultimate say, based on evidence presented to them, as to whether such probable cause exists. The Bush administration avoided these legal strictures against investigative or preventive detentions through the use of arrests for immigration law violations and "material witness" warrants. At the same time, it avoided or limited the ability of detainees to avail themselves of protections against arbitrary detention, including through meaningful judicial review.

Immediately after the September 11 attacks, the Department of Justice began a hit-or-miss process of questioning thousands of non-citizens, primarily foreign-born Muslim men, who it thought or guessed might have information about or connections to terrorist activity. At least 1,200 non-citizens were subsequently arrested and incarcerated, 752 of whom were charged with immigration violations.[6] These so-called "special interest" immigration detainees were presumed guilty of links to terrorism and incarcerated for months until the government "cleared" them of such connections. By February 2002 the Department of Justice acknowledged that most of the original "special interest" detainees were no longer of interest to its anti-terrorist efforts, and none was indicted for crimes related to the September 11 attacks. Most were deported for visa violations.

In effect, the Department of Justice used administrative proceedings under the immigration law as a proxy to detain and interrogate terrorism suspects without affording them the rights and protections that the US criminal system provides. The safeguards for immigration detainees are considerably fewer than for criminal suspects, and the Bush administration worked to weaken the safeguards that do exist. Human Rights Watch and other groups have documented the various ways the administration ran roughshod over the rights of these special interest detainees.[7] In June 2003, the Department of Justice's Office of the Inspector General released a comprehensive report on the treatment of the September 11 detainees which confirmed a pattern of abuses and delays for the "detainees, who were denied bond and the opportunity to leave the country…. For many detainees, this resulted in their continued detention in harsh conditions of confinement."[8]

For example, unlike criminal suspects, immigration detainees have no right to court-appointed counsel, although they do have a right to seek private counsel at their own expense. But in the case of the September 11 detainees, public officials placed numerous obstacles in the way of obtaining legal representation.[9] Detainees were not informed of their right to counsel or were discouraged from exercising that right. The Immigration and Naturalization Service (INS), a division of the US Department of Justice,[10] failed to inform attorneys where their clients were confined or when hearings were scheduled. Detainees in some facilities were permitted one weekly phone call, even to find or speak to an attorney; a call that did not go through nonetheless counted as the one permissible call. Not having prompt access to lawyers, these "special interest" detainees were unable to protest violations of immigration rules to which they were subjected, including being held for weeks without charges (some detainees were held for months before charges were filed). The government never revealed the alleged links to terrorism that prompted their arrest, leaving them unable to prove their innocence. The government also took advantage of the lack of counsel to conduct interrogations that typically addressed criminal as well as immigration matters (under criminal law, suspects have the right to have an attorney present during custodial interrogations, including free legal counsel if necessary).

In most immigration proceedings where non-citizens have violated the provisions of their visa, their detention is short. They will have a bond hearing relatively quickly after charges have been filed, and unless there is reason to believe the detainee is a danger to the community or will abscond, immigration judges will permit the detainee to be released on bond. With regard to the special interest detainees, however, the Department of Justice adopted several policies and practices to ensure they were denied release until it cleared them of terrorism links. For example, under immigration procedure, immigration judges do not automatically review whether there is probable cause for detention; hearings are not scheduled until after charges have been filed. The government's delay of weeks, and in some cases months, in filing charges had the practical effect of creating long delays in judicial review of the detentions. Additionally, the government urged immigration judges to set absurdly high bonds which the detainee could not possibly pay or simply to deny bond, arguing that the detainee should remain in custody until the government was able to rule out the possibility of links to or knowledge of the September 11 attacks.

The INS also issued a new rule that permitted it to keep a detainee in custody if the initial bond was more than $10,000, even if an immigration judge ordered him released; since the INS sets the initial bond amount, this rule gave the Department of Justice the means to ensure detainees would be kept in custody. In addition, there were cases in which the Department of Justice refused to release a special interest detainee even if a judge ordered the release because the detainee had not yet been "cleared" of connections to terrorism. Indeed, the INS continued to hold some detainees even after they had been ordered to be deported because of lack of "clearance" even though the INS is required to remove non-citizens expeditiously, and in any event within 90 days of a deportation order, as required by statute. In short, through these and other mechanisms, the immigration process to which the special interest detainees were subjected effectively reversed the presumption of innocence—non-citizens detained for immigration law violations were kept jailed until the government concluded they had no ties to criminal terrorist activities. As a result, special interest detainees remained in detention for an average of 80 days, and in some cases up to eight months, while they waited for the FBI to clear them of links to terrorism.

The long delays were endured by non-citizens who were picked up by chance by the FBI or INS as well as those the government actually had reason to believe might have a link to terrorism. Once a person was labeled of "special interest," there were no procedures by which those who in fact were of no interest could be processed more quickly. As the Office of the Inspector General noted, the lengthy investigations "had enormous ramifications," since detainees "languished" in prison while waiting for their names to be cleared.[11]

Despite the Inspector General's scathing criticism of the government's treatment of the detainees, the Department of Justice was unrepentant, issuing a public statement that it makes "no apologies for finding every legal way possible to protect the American public from further terrorist attacks.... The consequences of not doing so could mean life or death."[12] As of October 2003, the Executive Branch had adopted only two of the Inspector General's 21 recommendations designed to prevent a repetition of the problems documented.

SECRET ARRESTS AND HEARINGS OF SPECIAL INTEREST DETAINEES

History leaves little doubt that when a government deprives persons of their liberty in secret, human rights and justice are threatened. In the United States, detentions for violations of immigration laws are traditionally public. Nevertheless, of the 1,200 people reported arrested in connection with the post-September 11 investigations in the United States, approximately 1,000 were detained in secret.[13] The government released the names of some 100 detained on criminal charges, but it has refused to release the names, location of detention, lawyers' names, and other important information about those held on immigration charges. Even now, it refuses to release the names of men who have long since been deported.

The public secrecy surrounding the detentions had a very real and negative impact on detainees' ability to defend themselves. It made it difficult for family members and lawyers to track the location of the detainees, who were frequently moved; it prevented legal services organizations from contacting detainees who might need representation; and it prevented organizations such as Human Rights Watch from getting in touch with detainees directly and talking to them about how they were treated during their arrests and detentions.

On October 29, 2001, Human Rights Watch and other groups sought the names of the detainees, their lawyers' names, and their places of detention under the US Freedom of Information Act (FOIA)— legislation that mandates government disclosure of information subject to certain narrowly defined exceptions. The Department of Justice denied the request. When Human Rights Watch and the other groups went to court to challenge the government's denial, the government insisted that the release of the names would threaten national security, speculating about possible scenarios of harm that could flow if the names were public. For example, it asserted that revealing the names would provide terrorists with a road map to the government's anti-terrorism efforts. This argument appeared particularly specious since it was unlikely that a sophisticated terrorist organization would fail to know that its members were in the custody of the US government, especially since detainees were free to contact whomever they wished.

A federal district court rejected the government's arguments for secrecy in August 2002 and ordered the release of the identities of all those detained in connection with the September 11 investigation. The judge called the secret arrests "odious to a democratic society—and profoundly antithetical to the bedrock values that characterize a free and open one such as ours."[14] However, in June 2003 the court of appeals reversed that decision. In a passionate dissent, one appellate judge noted:

> Congress ... chose ... to require meaningful judicial review of all government [FOIA] exemption claims .... For all its concern about the separation-of-powers principles at issue in this case, the court violates those principles by essentially abdicating its responsibility to apply the law as Congress wrote it.[15]

In October 2003, Human Rights Watch and 21 other organizations asked the US Supreme Court to overturn the appellate decision and to compel the Department of Justice to release the names. Meanwhile, the Department of Justice imposed blanket secrecy over every minute of 600 immigration hearings involving special interest detainees so that even immediate family members were denied access to the hearings. The policy of secrecy extended even to notice of the hearing itself: courts were ordered not to give out any information about whether a case was on the docket or scheduled for a hearing.[16] The Justice Department has never presented a cogent rationale for this closure policy, particularly since deportation proceedings are typically limited to the simple inquiry of whether the individual is lawfully present or has any legal reason to remain in the United States, an inquiry that should not require disclosure of any classified information. Moreover, if the Justice Department sought to present classified information during a hearing, simply closing those portions of the proceedings where such material was presented could have protected national security.

Newspapers brought two lawsuits challenging the secret hearings, alleging the blanket closure policy violated the public's constitutional right to know "what their government is up to." In one case in August 2002, an appellate court struck down the policy. The court minced no words in explaining just what was threatened by the government's insistence on secrecy, stating that:

> The Executive Branch seeks to uproot people's lives, outside the public eye, and behind a closed door. Democracies die behind closed doors. The First Amendment, through a free press, protects the people's right to know that their government acts fairly, lawfully, and accurately in deportation proceedings. When government begins closing doors, it selectively controls information rightfully belonging to the people.[17]

The government declined to appeal this decision to the Supreme Court.

In the second case, a federal appeals court upheld the closures, finding that the need for national security was greater than the right of access to deportation hearings. The Supreme Court declined to review that decision in May 2003. Significantly, in its brief filed in opposition to the Supreme Court hearing the case, the US government distanced itself from the blanket closure policy, stating that it was not conducting any more secret hearings and that its policies relating to secret hearings were under review and would "likely" be changed.

MATERIAL WITNESS WARRANTS

In addition to immigration charges, the Bush administration has used so-called material witness warrants to subject individuals of interest to its terrorism investigation to "preventive detention" and to minimize judicial scrutiny of these detentions. US law permits detention of a witness when his or her testimony is material to a criminal proceeding, and when the witness presents a risk of absconding before testifying. According to the Department of Justice, the government has used the material witness law to secure the detention of less than 50 people (it has refused to release the exact number) in connection with the September 11 investigations.[18]

The US government has obtained judicial arrest warrants for material witnesses by arguing that they have information to present to the grand juries investigating the crimes of September 11. The available information on these cases suggests that the government was misusing the material witness warrants to secure the detention of people it believed might have knowledge about September 11—but who could not be held on immigration charges and against whom there was insufficient evidence to bring criminal charges. In many of the cases, the witnesses were never presented to a grand jury but were detained for weeks or months, under punitive prison conditions, while the government interrogated them and continued its investigations.[19]

The *Washington Post* reported in November 2002 that of the 44 men it identified as being detained as material witnesses since September 11, 2001, nearly half had never been called to testify in front of a grand jury. In some cases, men originally held as material witnesses were ultimately charged with crimes, strengthening the suspicion that the government was using the material witness designation as a pretext until it had time to accumulate the evidence necessary to bring criminal charges. A number of the witnesses languished in jail for months or were eventually deported, based on criminal and immigration charges unrelated to September 11 that were supported by evidence the government gathered while detaining them as material witnesses.

Material witness warrants are supposed to ensure the presentation of testimony in a criminal proceeding where the witness cannot otherwise be subpoenaed to testify and where there is a serious risk that the witness will abscond rather than testify. In September 11 cases, at least some courts have accepted with little scrutiny the government's allegations that these requirements are satisfied. At the insistence of the government, the courts have also agreed to restrict access by the detainees' lawyers to the government's evidence, making it difficult if not impossible for the lawyers to object to the necessity of detention. For example, in some cases lawyers were only able to review the evidence supporting the request for the warrant quickly in court and they were unable to go over the information carefully with their clients before the hearing started. In addition, the government has argued in at least some cases that the mostly male Arab and Muslim witnesses were flight risks simply because they are non-citizens (even though some are lawful permanent residents), and have family abroad. The government's argument amounted to no more than an astonishing assumption that millions of non-citizens living in the United States with family living abroad cannot be counted on to comply with US law and to testify under a subpoena.

The Bush administration has held the material witnesses in jail for extended periods of time, in some cases for months, and subjected them to the same conditions of confinement as given to accused or convicted criminals. Indeed, some have been held in solitary confinement and subjected to security measures typically reserved for extremely dangerous persons.

The Department of Justice has argued that it must keep all information pertaining to material witnesses confidential because "disclosing such specific information would be detrimental to the war on terror and the investigation of the September 11 attacks," and that US law requires that all information related to grand jury proceedings be kept under seal.[20] It has refused to identify which information must specifically be kept secret because of its relevance to grand jury proceedings and national security interests; instead, it has not only kept witnesses' identities secret, but has also refused to disclose their number, the grounds on which they were detained, and the length and location of their detention. To shroud the circumstances of detention of innocent witnesses in secrecy raises serious concerns. As one court recently stated: "To withhold that information could create public perception that an unindicted member of the community has been arrested and secretly imprisoned by the government."[21]

PRESIDENTIAL EXERCISE OF WARTIME POWERS

Since September 11 the Bush administration has maintained that the president's wartime power as commander-in-chief allows him to detain indefinitely and without charges anyone he designates as an "enemy combatant" in the "war against terrorism." On this basis the government is currently holding three men incommunicado in military brigs in the United States and some 660 non-citizens at Guantánamo Bay in

Why were family members of the most wanted man in America not detained for questioning?

AN ALTERNATIVE STORY TIES THE ALLEGED TERRORISTS TO THE CIA AND PAKISTAN'S ISI

It is most likely that Pakistan's Inter Services Intelligence (ISI) was directly involved in 9/11.[16] The links between al Qaeda, Pakistan's ISI and the CIA, and between the ISI, Osama bin Laden and the Taliban axis are a matter of public record. The CIA also has close cooperative links with Mossad (Israeli intelligence) which also may have played an important role in 9/11. Pakistan has long been a supporter of al Qaeda. The ISI has been a mechanism by which the CIA indirectly channeled support to al Qaeda and has been used by successive US administrations as a "go-between." Pakistan's military intelligence apparatus constitutes the core institutional support to both Osama bin Laden's al Qaeda and the Taliban. Without this institutional support, there would have been no Taliban government in Kabul. In turn, without the support of the US government, there would be no powerful military intelligence apparatus in Pakistan.

It was reported that ISI's director-general, General Mahmoud Ahmad, had funneled $100,000 to the alleged lead hijacker, Mohammed Atta, shortly before September 11. The US government protected him, and itself, by asking him to resign after the discovery, thus blocking a further inquiry and a potential scandal. In the wake of 9/11, the Bush administration consciously sought the "cooperation" of the ISI, which had been supporting and abetting Osama bin Laden and the Taliban. In other words, the Bush administration's relations with Pakistan's ISI, including its "consultations" with General Mahmoud Ahmad in the week prior to September 11, raise the issues of cover-up and complicity. While Ahmad was talking to US officials at the CIA and the Pentagon, the ISI allegedly had contacts with the 9/11 terrorists.

THOSE WHO BENEFITED THE MOST FROM 9/11

The 9/11 attacks came at an extremely fortuitous time for the Bush administration, the Pentagon, the CIA, the FBI, the weapons industry, and the oil industry, all of which have benefited immensely from this tragedy, as has Israel. It is worth noting the astute observations of Canadian social philosopher John McMurtry: "To begin with, the forensic principle of 'who most benefits from the crime?' clearly points in the direction of the Bush administration. ... The more you review the connections and the sweeping lapse of security across so many coordinates, the more the lines point backwards"]to the White House]. If you add "follow the money," one trail goes from the CIA to Pakistan's ISI to al Qaeda, and another trail goes from US taxpayers to particular players in the military-industrial complex connected to the Bush administration.

The 9/11 disaster has resulted in power and profit at home and abroad by both the bin Laden and the Bush families. There are significant business ties between bin Laden and senior members of the Bush administration through the Carlyle Group, the giant private and secretive investment firm managing some $14 billion in assets, including many defense-related companies. Carlyle employs George Bush Sr, and has long-standing financial ties to the bin Laden family. So while there is compelling evidence that Osama bin Laden has not broken from his family, it is also a matter of record that the Bush administration is in turn very significantly tied to the same family. Reports have emerged that the Carlyle Group, Halliburton, and many other firms with ties to the Bush administration have profited immensely from the wars in Afghanistan and Iraq and from the militarization of US foreign policy.

Israel is the regional watchdog for the West but is also dependent on the US for its security. Clearly it benefits from the US occupation of one of its most feared enemies. It may also now share in some of the benefits from the world's second largest oil reserve.

Two further arguments support the contention that the Bush administration's complicity in 9/11, but the details are given in other chapters of this volume. First, it is recognized that the wars on Afghanistan and Iraq were planned prior to 9/11 as revealed in documents from the Project for a New American Century and in Zbigniew Brzezinski's "The Grand Chessboad." Second, there are well-documented precedents for government acts of complicity and fabrications.[17]

LIES, SECRECY, AND COVER-UP

There has never been a single event in the history of the US republic which has received more media coverage. Moreover, there were 2,952 people killed in the 2001 World Trade Center attacks, more civilian deaths on a single day than at any other time. In spite of the unprecedented magnitude of death and destruction in New York on 9/11, the US government spent only $600,000 for its single study of the causes for the Twin Towers collapses. Compare this to the $40 million that was spent investigating Bill Clinton's activities with Monica Lewinksy in 1988–99 and the only rational conclusion is that there is no desire on